THE BEATLES

A REFERENCE & VALUE GUIDE

MICHAEL STERN • BARBARA CRAWFORD • HOLLIS LAMON

COLLECTOR BOOKS
A Division of Schroeder Publishing

The current values in this book should be used only as a guide. They are not intended to set prices, which vary from one section of the country to another. Auction prices as well as dealer prices vary greatly and are affected by condition as well as demand. Neither the Authors nor the Publisher assumes responsibility for any losses that might be incurred as a result of consulting this guide.

Searching For A Publisher?

We are always looking for knowledgeable people considered to be experts within their fields. If you feel that there is a real need for a book on your collectible subject and have a large comprehensive collection, contact us.

COLLECTOR BOOKS
P.O. Box 3009
Paducah, Kentucky 42002-3009

Additional copies of this book may be ordered from:

COLLECTOR BOOKS
P.O. Box 3009
Paducah, Kentucky 42002-3009

@$17.95. Add $2.00 for postage and handling.

1 2 3 4 5 6 7 8 9 0

Table of Contents

Acknowledgments

To Barbara Crawford whose photography makes the pictures come to life.

To all the Beatle enthusiasts and collectors who gave us constant encouragement.

To Bob Gottuso, (BoJo) who sold us many of the items pictured in the book and whose advice and knowledge was invaluable.

Introduction

The Beatles influenced and changed a whole generation. They created rock 'n' roll and established rock music as an art form. The Beatles left a mark on the millions of the kids who saw and heard them. The Beatles and their music are synonymous with the vibrant times of the 1960's. They did more to influence and impact the youth of the 1960's than did anyone else. The Beatles were trend setters from fashion to hairstyles.

I grew up in this era and remember vividly watching their live appearance on the "Ed Sullivan Show" and taping it on my reel to reel. I experienced their music and my life seemed to mirror their changing music as I grew from adolescence to adulthood. From "Meet the Beatles" to "Sgt. Peppers" to the "White Album," I was there with them.

This book is not a history of the Beatles. It is an identification and value guide to the artifacts of the 1960's that were created because of them. These items of memorabilia encompassed almost every type of object. If it could be sold, some company created the product with the Beatles image somewhere on it. If you were one who grew up to the Beatles' music, you will be able to relate to each piece of memorabilia, but I assure you, you will remember only a handful of these items.

The field of rock 'n' roll collecting has come of age and the Beatles, as they did with their music, are leading the way. Today with Hard Rock Cafes being built in most major cities and Beatlefest being held all over the world, there is a refocusing on the Beatles and the collectibles that were made to promote them. All major auction houses, including Christies and Sotheby's, now have rock 'n' roll auctions. In fact, John Lennon's Rolls Royce sold for $2,292,600 at Sotheby's in New York, which put its price in the top ten car prices in the world.

This book will not deal with records or with fan magazines. To me both of these areas are collecting fields unto themselves. This book deals in licensed products that could be bought in stores worldwide during the times that they were produced.

The memorabilia in this book was brought to market in three different time frames. Each will have its own section in the book. The largest concentration of Beatles memorabilia was created and produced in 1964 and 1965 when the Beatles were in their heyday. Then in 1968, with the release of the movie, *Yellow Submarine,* stores were stocked with a whole new product line just in time for Christmas. The third wave of merchandise was when Apple Productions was formed and consisted of promotional pieces.

The book also features cels (*Yellow Submarine* movie celluloids) which is a field of increasing popularity and one in which prices are escalating rapidly.

The collecting of Beatle memorabilia is the collecting of an art form and the appreciation of the prices of this art form parallels the increase in the values of all forms of art work. It could be said that collecting is like buying quality stocks and bonds, an excellent investment that increases in value annually. The added value is that whereas stocks and bonds are tucked away in a safe or vault, your Beatle collectibles can be displayed and enjoyed on a daily basis.

All of the photographs in this book are taken from the collection of Barbara Crawford. Barbara has been a Beatle fanatic for many years and can now boast of one of the premier collections in the world. Her devotion and dedication to achieving this goal has made this book a reality.

Our hope is that this book will help the novice collectors in broadening their scope so that when acquiring a piece of Beatle memorabilia, it can be dated and its price put into perspective.

— Michael Stern

Pricing Information

This value guide for Beatles collectibles is to be used as a point of reference before buying or selling an item. Any value guide tends to be subjective in nature, and we've used the sources available to us to arrive at what we think are accurate price points in today's marketplace. The Beatles collectible market can change dramatically in a very short span of time.

We have determined the values for each item based on a number of factors and sources:

1. What we have paid for each item.
2. Auction catalogs.
3. Mail auction price realized lists.
4. Toy and doll show prices.
5. Antique trader ads.

We feel the values suggested are excellent estimates of what each item is actually worth. The basic law of economics — supply and demand — can shoot holes through any value guide. "The worth of a collectible is what someone will pay for it," is an adage which is still prevalent for today's collectors.

The following descriptions relate to the condition of the item and how they are priced accordingly.

Good Condition

An item in good condition is in working order, has been used, shows general wear and tear. The item must look fairly clean with little or no rust.

Excellent, Mint Condition

Excellent means the item is clean and looks as if it has never been used. It is complete and all functions are operative. Mint applies to mint in the box (MIB) and means the item is in its original package. In many cases, the box is worth more than the item itself.

Each item has been priced as it appears in the picture (with box, with tag, with label.)

CHAPTER ONE
Early Beatles Memorabilia

This chapter is the largest in the book. It deals with merchandise produced in the early years of the Beatles and their rise to success. Most of the items pictured in this chapter were manufactured in 1964 and 1965.

Brian Epstein, the manager of the Beatles, realized that he could generate substantial profits by selling thousands of different items bearing the Beatles pictures. He knew the Beatles were a marketable commodity. He formed the North End Music Stores to license and approve all Beatles merchandise. They wanted quality products so their seal of approval was the words "NEMS" which stood for North End Music Stores and was put on licensed products. If the items were produced in the United States, they were marked SELTAEB which is Beatles spelled backwards.

For a group that stayed together only seven years, there was an incredible amount of merchandise produced. There was an endless supply and variety from many different countries.

Beware — counterfeits do exist and many have used the "NEMS" marking. Many of the counterfeits are items easily made such as buttons, playing cards, and soap bubbles. When an item's validity is contingent on just a label, caution is advised.

The key to the pricing of an item is condition, condition, condition!

Plastic Beatles Placemat.

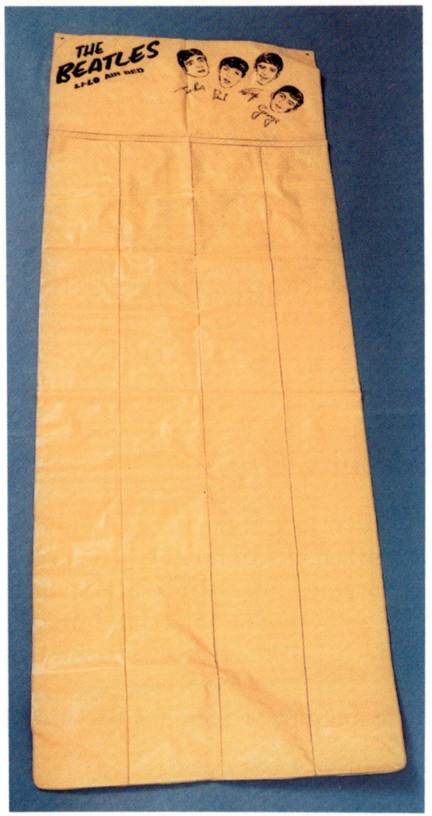

Plate 1. *Airbed* is a very rare piece manufactured only in England by the Li-Lo Company. It is made of vinyl and can be inflated. Good, $1,000.00; Excellent/Mint, $1,200.00.

Plate 2. *Assignment Book* was manufactured by Select-O-Pack. It is vinyl and has two note pads included — Lesson Assignments and Classroom Notes. Good, $150.00; Excellent/Mint, $225.00.

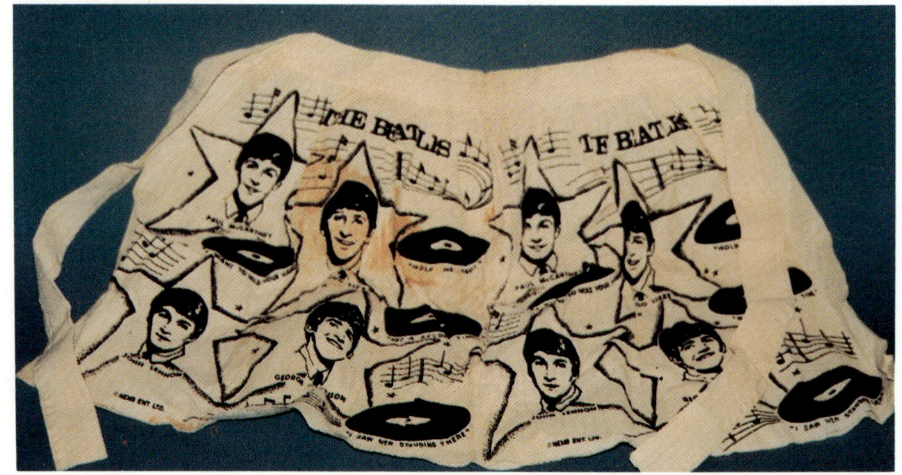

Plate 3. *Apron* is a NEMS ENT, Ltd. product. It is made of a paper-like fiber. Good, $350.00; Excellent/Mint, $400.00.

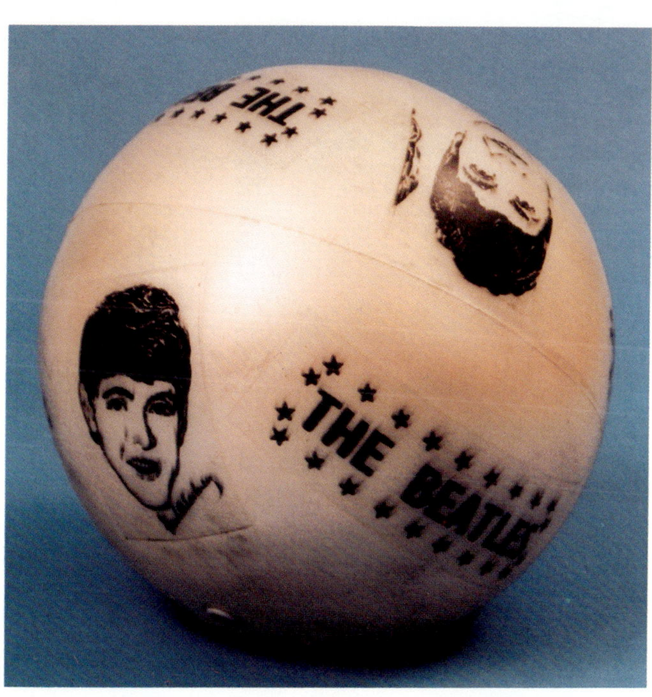

Plate 4. *Ball* is white rubber and is inflated. It is 8" in diameter. Good, $600.00; Excellent/Mint, $700.00.

Plate 5. *Ball* is one of the few known to exist in its original packaging. When it is inflated, it is 14" in diameter. It was made by the Seltaeb Company and is made of all rubber. Good, $800; Excellent/Mint, $900.

Plate 6. *Balloons* were made by the United Industries of Southington, Connecticut. This item can be found in a variety of colors. The group shot is pictured on each balloon. Good, $50.00; Excellent/Mint, $60.00.

Plate 7. *Bamboo Plates* were produced by the Bamboo Tray Specialist Company. The scene pictured is from *A Hard Days Night*. Sizes pictured left to right are 11" and 6" in diameter. Good, $120.00; Excellent/Mint,

Plate 8. *Bamboo Plate* is the third size and largest. It is 12" in diameter. Good, $120.00; Excellent/Mint, $145.00.

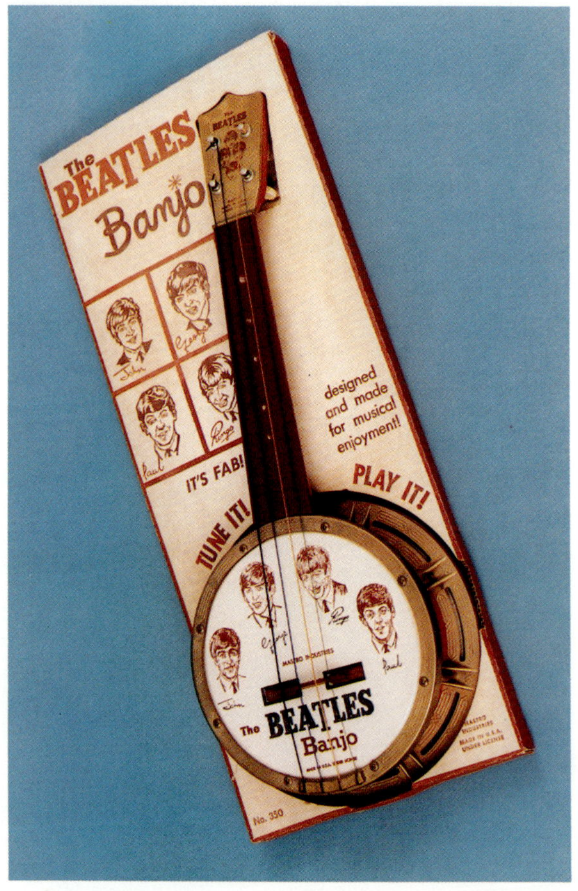

Plate 9. *Banjo* is one of the hardest items to find especially in its original cardboard container. It was manufactured by Mastro and is 22" long. The banjo is one of the most sought after items by collectors. It's Fab! Good, $2,000.00, Excellent/Mint, $2,500.00.

Plate 10. *Beach Towel* was made for Cannon. It shows the Beatles in old fashioned bathing suits. Good, $100.00; Excellent/Mint, $125.00.

Plate 11. *Bedsheets* are from the Whittier Hotel in Detroit. The Beatles used these sheets on September 6, 1964. There is one for each Beatle and they are attached to a letter of authenticity. Good, $75.00; Excellent/Mint, $100.00.

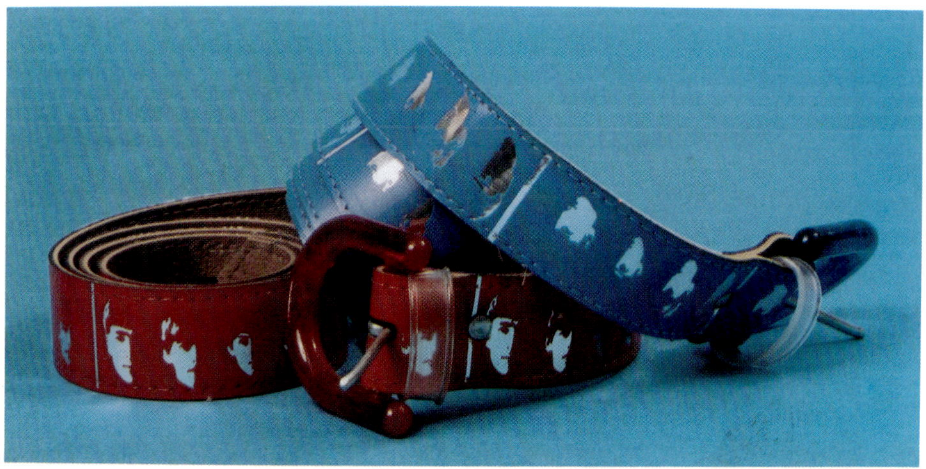

Plate 12. *Belts* are made of vinyl and can be found in a variety of colors. Good, $80.00; Excellent/Mint, $90.00.

Plate 13. *Belt Buckle* utilizes a black and white picture of the group surrounded by heavy metal. Good, $100.00; Excellent/Mint, $125.00.

Plate 14. *Binder* was produced by New York Looseleaf Corporation. This is the three ring variation. They were produced in various colors. Good, $100.00; Excellent/Mint, $125.00.

Plate 15. *Binder* in the rare purple color variation. Good, $150.00; Excellent/Mint, $175.00.

Plate 16. *Binder* in the turquoise variation. Good, $225.00; Excellent/Mint, $250.00.

Plate 17. *Binders* were produced in many sizes and hold variations. This is a three ring and two ring in the same color. Good, $100.00; Excellent/Mint, $125.00.

Plate 18. *Birth Certificates* are contained in cartoon-like booklets. Good, $75.00. Excellent/Mint, $100.00.

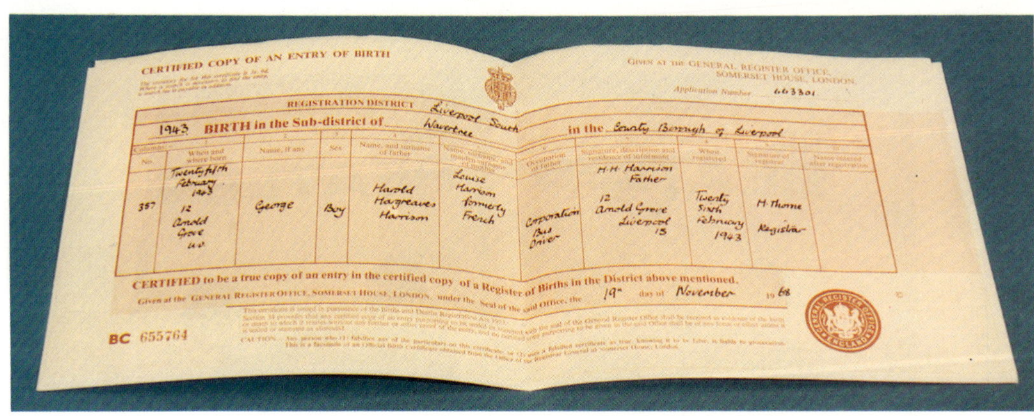

CERTIFIED COPY OF AN ENTRY OF BIRTH

GIVEN AT THE GENERAL REGISTER OFFICE, SOMERSET HOUSE, LONDON.

Application Number 663301

REGISTRATION DISTRICT Liverpool South

1943 BIRTH in the Sub-district of Wavertree in the County Borough of Liverpool

No.	When and where born	Name, if any	Sex	Name, and surname of father	[illegible]	Occupation of father	[illegible]	When registered	[illegible]	[illegible]
357	Twentyfifth February 1943 12 Arnold Grove U.D.	George	Boy	Harold Hargreaves Harrison	Louise Harrison formerly French	Corporation Bus Driver	H.H. Harrison Father 12 Arnold Grove Liverpool 15	Twenty Sixth February 1943	H. Thorne Registrar	

CERTIFIED to be a true copy of an entry in the certified copy of a Register of Births in the District above mentioned.

Given at the GENERAL REGISTER OFFICE, SOMERSET HOUSE, LONDON, under the Seal of the said Office, the 19th day of November 1968

BC 655764

Plate 19. *Birth Certificate* is an example of one of the birth certificates in the booklets. Good, $75.00; Excellent/Mint, $100.00.

Plate 20. *Birthday Card* was printed by American Greetings. Good, $35.00; Excellent/Mint, $40.00.

Plate 21. *Blanket* was produced by the Witney Company. It is 62" wide and 80" long. It is made of wool and fiber. Good, $400; Excellent/Mint, $450.00.

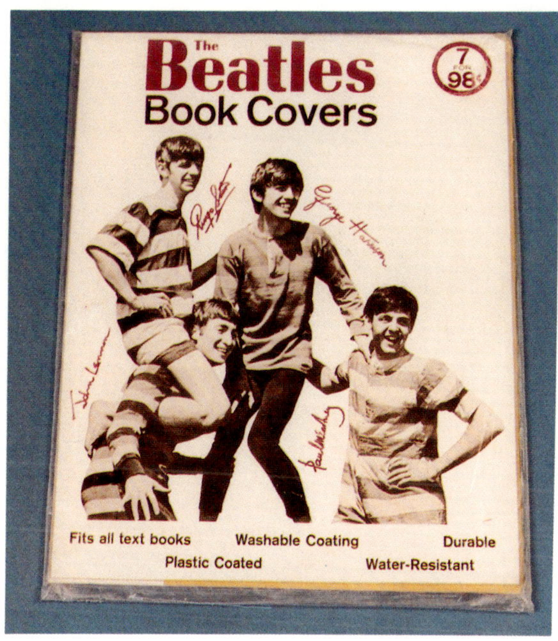

Plate 22. *Book Covers* were made by Book Covers, Inc. There are seven in the sealed package. Good, $110.00; Excellent/Mint, $120.00.

Plate 23. *Bongos* are one of the most difficult items to find. They were made by Mastro and are plastic with white skin on top. Good, $3,000.00; Excellent/Mint, $3,300.00.

Plate 24. *Booty Bag* is waterproof and made of clear plastic. It came with an insert that describes different uses. They can be carried in three different ways. Good, $150.00; Excellent/Mint, $165.00.

Plate 25. *Booty Bag* produced in another color variation. Good, $150.00; Excellent/Mint, $165.00.

Plate 26. *Bust* is of Ringo and was produced by Starfans. It is 6¼" tall and is made of hard rubber. There are no busts of the other Beatles. Good, $175.00; Excellent/Mint, $200.00.

Plate 27. *Brunch Bag* was made by Aladdin. It is made of vinyl and is much rarer than the metal lunch box. Good, $500.00; Excellent/Mint, $525.00.

Plate 28. *Bubble Bath* was produced by Colgate. Paul is 9" tall and his head unscrews to reveal contents. Good, $200.00; Excellent/Mint, $225.00.

Plate 29. *Bubble Bath* utilizes Ringo. For some unknown reason, Ringo and Paul were the only two Beatles to be used by Colgate as soap containers. Good, $200.00; Excellent/Mint, $225.00.

Plate 30. *Buttons* that were originally sold in gumball machines. They were made by Green Duck Company and measure 1". Good, $10.00; Excellent/Mint, $15.00.

Plate 31. *Buttons* pictured are the three sizes of one of the most common buttons. Good, $15.00; Excellent/Mint, $20.00.

Plate 32. *Buttons* are a blue variety of the 1" Green Duck Company button. Good, $10.00; Excellent/Mint, $15.00.

Plate 33. *Button* is 3 inches in diameter. Good, $15.00; Excellent/Mint, $20.00

Plate 34. *Buttons* are 1" and were sold in gumball machines. Good, $10.00; Excellent/Mint, $15.00.

Plate 35. *Buttons Display Card* is for the Flip Button set. Good, $600.00; Excellent/Mint, $650.00.

Plate 36. *Buttons* (The "I Love Series"). Good, $5.00; Excellent/Mint, $10.00.

Plate 39. *Buttons* are referred to as Flip Buttons and utilize flicker pictures. Good, $15.00; Excellent/Mint, $20.00.

Plate 38. *Button* is another example of a 3" button. Note the misspelling of Beatles. Good, $5.00. Excellent/Mint, $10.00.

Plate 37. *Button* is 3 inches in diameter. Good, $15.00; Excellent/Mint, $20.00.

Plate 40. *Buttons* with use of actual pictures. Good, $15.00; Excellent/Mint, $20.00.

Plate 41. *Button Display Card* used for fan club. Good, $250.00; Excellent/Mint, $300.00.

Plate 42. *Cake Decorations* are plastic heads used to decorate a cake. Good, $55.00; Excellent/Mint, $60.00.

Plate 43. *Cake Decorations* are made of plastic. Good, $25.00; Excellent/Mint, $30.00.

Plate 44. *Cake Decorations* can be found in a variety of sizes and poses. Good, $25.00; Excellent/Mint, $30.00.

Plate 45. *Calendar* is a very rare item. It has plastic knobs on the back to change the date. Good, $350.00; Excellent/Mint, $400.00.

Plate 46. *Calendar* is unusual in that it began to be sold in March, 1964, and that was the first month used. Good, $100.00; Excellent/Mint, $125.00.

Plate 47. *Calendar* using "Make a Date with the Beatles" theme is very rare. It is plastic and stands upright. There are knobs on the back so one can set the day of the week, month, and date. Good, $350.00; Excellent/Mint, $400.00.

Plate 48. *Calendar Cards* were produced by Louis F. Dow Company. They are plastic and have group or individuals pictures on front and specific month of 1964-1965 on back. Good, $40.00; Excellent/Mint, $45.00.

Plate 49. *Candy Dishes* were manufactured by Washington Pottery. Each is bordered with a gold trim. The Ringo dish is the only one with "The Beatles" written on the bottom. Good, $175.00; Excellent/Mint, $200.00.

Plate 50. *Candy Cigarette Boxes* were made by World Candies, Inc. The boxes are small measuring 1" x 2½". Each was made to hold two pieces of candy. There were many different boxes produced. Good, $110.00; Excellent/Mint, $120.00.

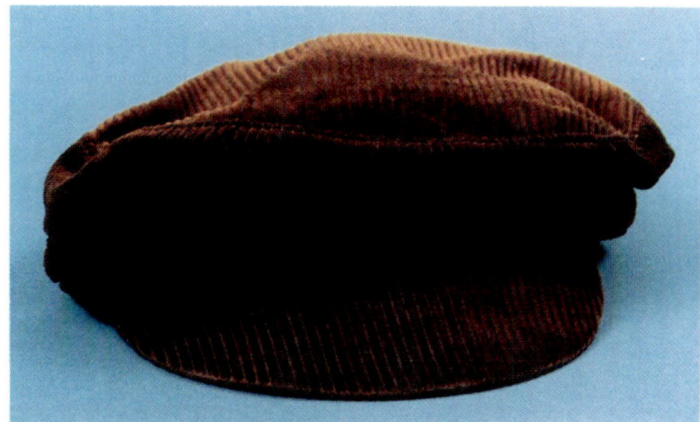

Plate 51. *Cap* is known as the "Ringo Cap" and is so designated on the label inside. This Ringo Cap is brown and made of corduroy. Good, $150.00; Excellent/Mint, $175.00.

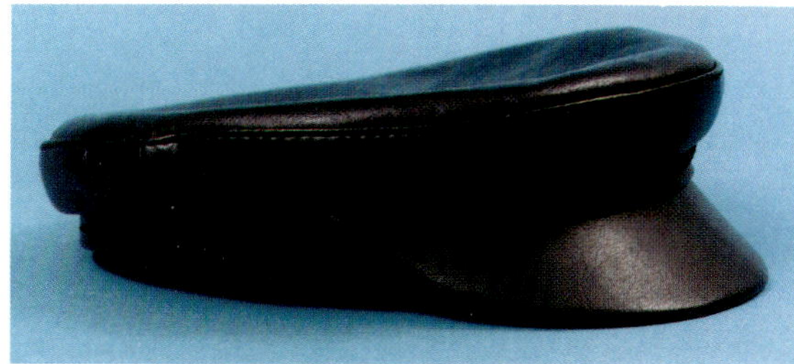

Plate 52. *Cap* is another variation of the "Ringo Cap." It is made of leather. Good, $150.00; Excellent/Mint, $175.00.

Plate 53. *Cap* is another variation of the "Ringo Cap." Good, $150.00; Excellent/Mint, $175.00.

Plate 54. *Cellophane Tape* was made in San Juan by the Starlight Company. The tape is cellophane and self adhesive. This is 5½". This was unknown to exist until March, 1992, and has never been pictured before. Good, $350.00; Excellent/Mint, $400.00.

Plate 55. *Carrying Case* was produced by AirFlite. It is made of vinyl and has a plastic handle. All the AirFlite products are very desirable. Good, $650.00; Excellent/Mint, $700.00.

Plate 56. *Carrying Case* is another color variation of the difficult to find AirFlite product line. Good, $650.00; Excellent/Mint, $700.00.

Plate 58. *China (Biscuit Plate)* was made by Washington Pottery and has an indenture for a cup. Good, $140.00; Excellent/Mint, $150.00.

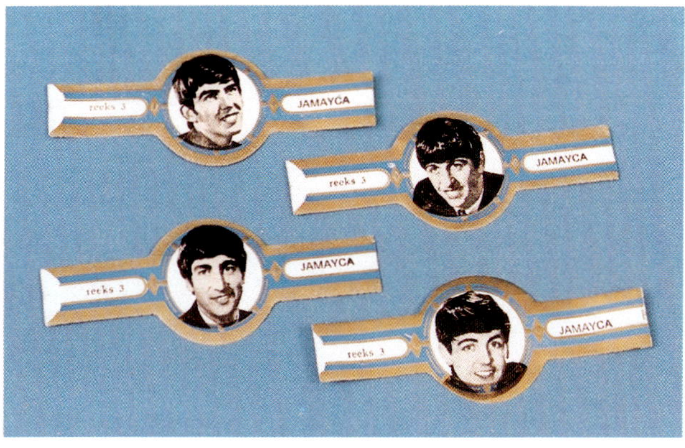

Plate 57. *Cigar Bands* were made in Jamaica, thus demonstrating that the Beatles' faces were used on everything. Good, $80.00; Excellent/Mint, $90.00.

Plate 60. *Cellophane Tape* is the smaller and known version. It is the only Beatle item that was made exclusively in San Juan. Good, $200.00; Excellent/Mint, $225.00.

Plate 59. *China (Plate)* was made by Washington Pottery and is 7" in diameter. Good, $110.00; Excellent/Mint, $120.00.

Plate 61. *Cigar Bands* were made in Germany. Note the names are incorrect. Good, $80.00; Excellent/Mint, $90.00.

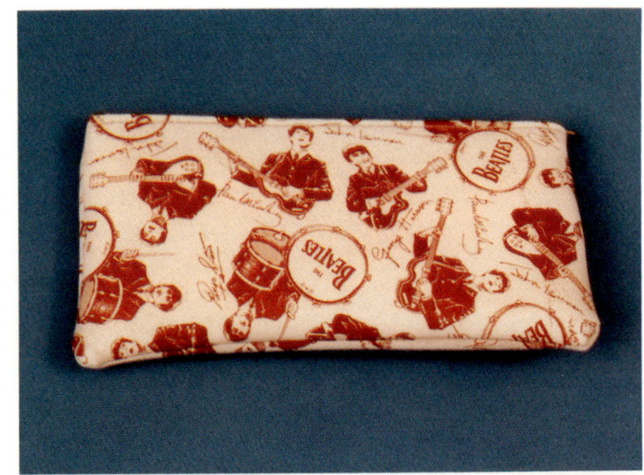

Plate 62. *Clutch Purses* were made of different materials. This one is made of vinyl and has a zippered top. Good, $175.00; Excellent/Mint, $200.00.

Plate 63. *Clothes Tags* were made by Ninth Street Limited and were used on mod fashion clothing. Good, $60.00; Excellent/Mint, $65.00.

Plate 64. *Clutch Purse* is made of cloth and shows its original tag. It has a brown strap as its handle. Good, $225.00; Excellent/Mint, $250.00.

Plate 65. *Clutch Purse* is made of vinyl and has a zippered top with a leather-like strap. Good, $300.00; Excellent/Mint, $325.00.

Plate 66. *Clutch Purse* in a different color. Good, $300.00; Excellent/Mint, $325.00.

Plate 67. *Clutch Purse* made in a hard-to-find orange color. Good, $300.00; Excellent/Mint, $325.00.

Plate 68. *Clutch Purse* in the rare brown color. Good, $300.00; Excellent/Mint, $325.00.

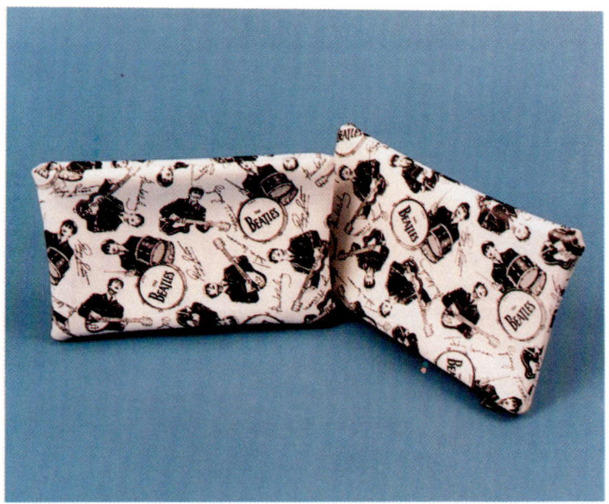

Plate 69. *Clutch Purses* are another variation utilizing different logo patterns. Good, $300.00; Excellent/Mint, $325.00.

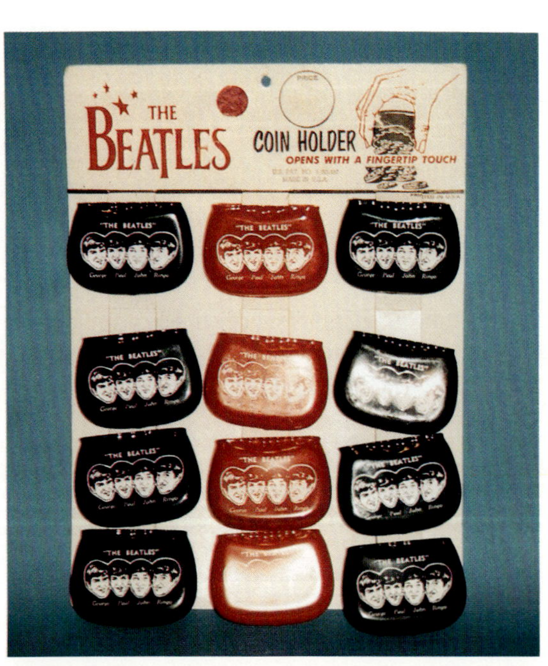

Plate 70. *Coin Holder Display Card* contains 12 coin holders. They are black and red. Good, $700.00; Excellent/Mint, $725.00.

Plate 71. *Coin Purse* is made of vinyl and can be found in various colors. Good, $35.00; Excellent/Mint, $40.00.

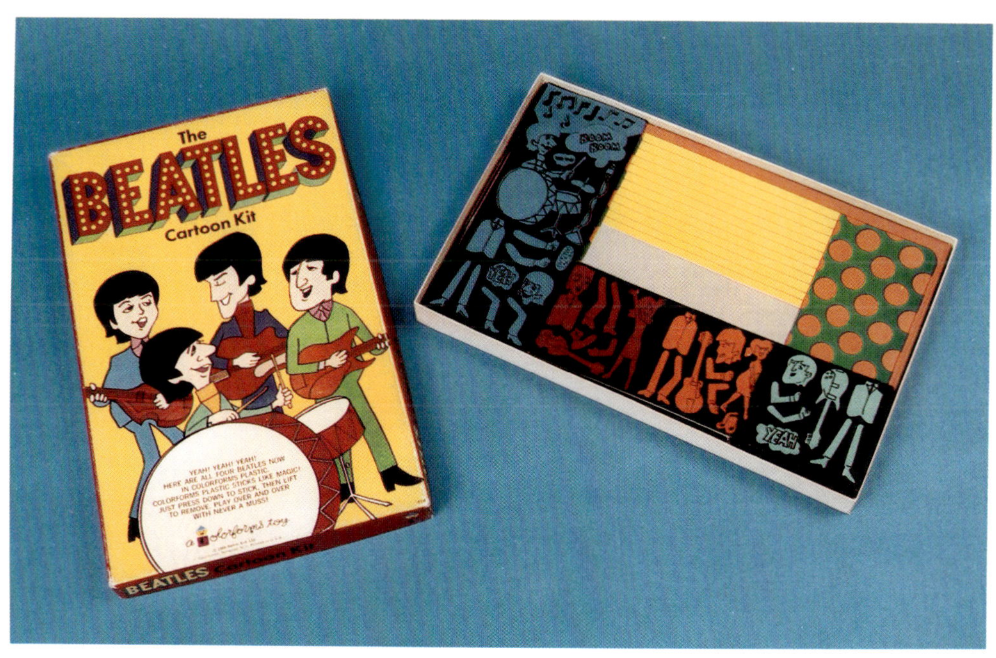

Plate 72. *Colorforms* were made in 1966 by Colorforms. This kit utilized the Beatles and their instruments and a stage to place the pieces. A difficult toy to find in excellent condition. Good, $500.00; Excellent/Mint, $550.00.

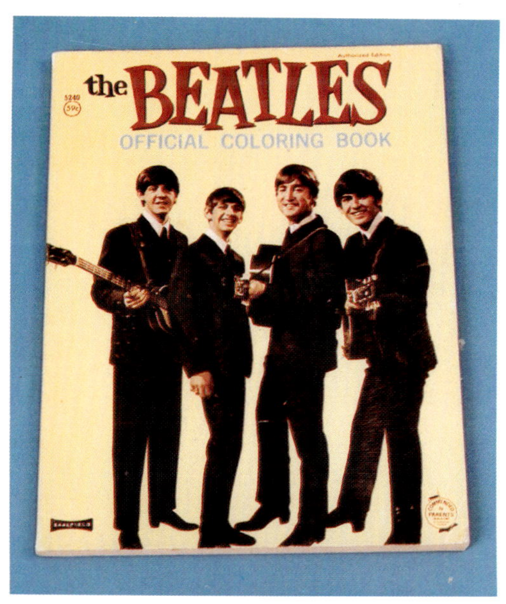

Plate 73. *Coloring Book* was produced by Saalfield. Good, $60.00; Excellent/Mint, $75.00.

Plate 74. *Coloring Set* was manufactured by Kilfix and included five numbered portraits to be painted by the number. Good, $1,300.00; Excellent/Mint, $1,500.00.

Plate 75. *Comic Book* using "Meet the Beatles" story as the main theme. Good, $50.00; Excellent/Mint, $60.00.

Plate 76. *Comb* was produced by Lido Toys. It is plastic and unusually large for a comb. It measures 14½". It was produced in a variety of colors. Good, $70.00; Excellent/Mint, $80.00.

Plate 77. *Comic Book* using the Beatles saving a romance as the story line. Good, $50.00; Excellent/Mint, $60.00.

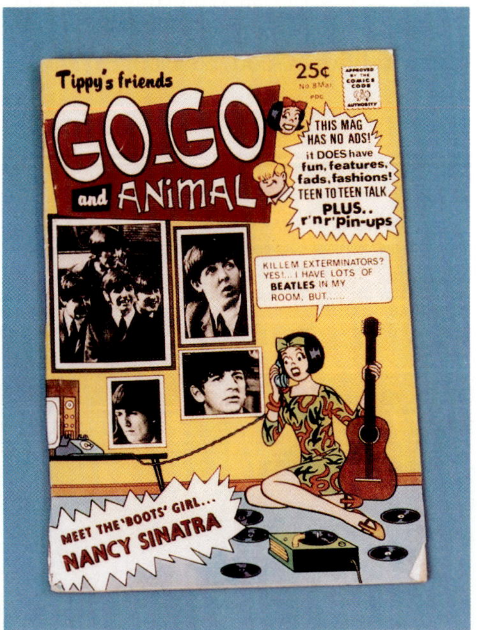

Plate 78. *Comic Book* using Beatles photographs on cover. Good, $50.00; Excellent/Mint, $60.00.

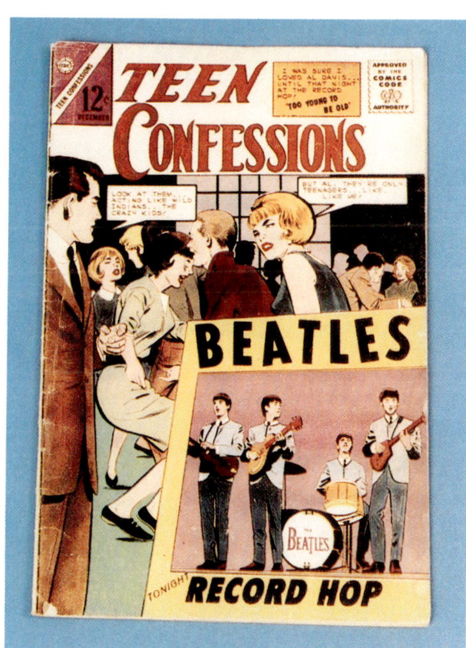

Plate 79. *Comic Book* using the Beatles as a story line. Good, $50.00; Excellent/ Mint, $60.00.

Plate 80. *Compact* was made only in England and is a very rare piece of memorabilia. The one pictured still has the make-up in tact. The compact itself is brass. Good, $550.00; Excellent/Mint, $600.00.

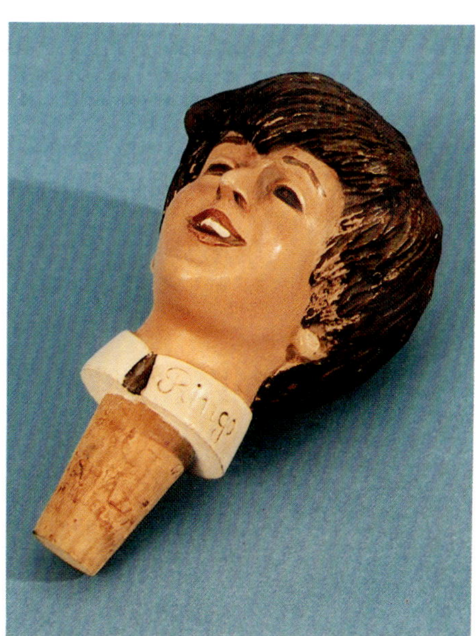

Plate 81. *Corkstopper* is a very rare piece of memorabilia. The head is wooden. Ringo may be the only Beatle used for this product. Good, $600.00; Excellent/Mint, $625.00.

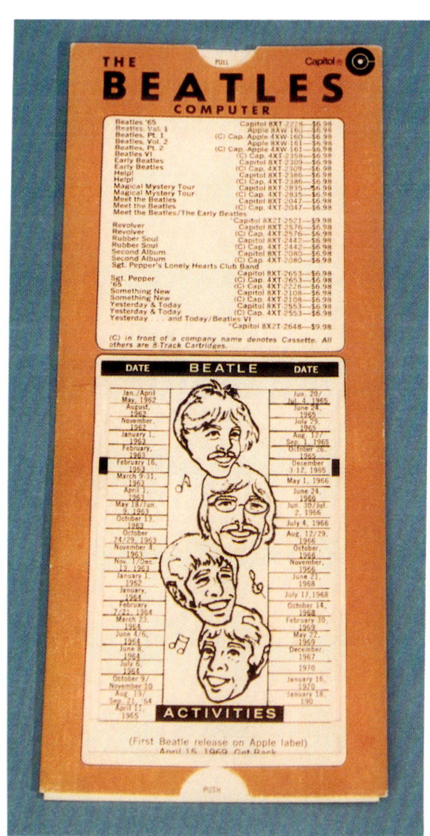

Plate 82. *Computer* is a later item made in 1970 for use by Capital Records. It is loaded with facts about the Beatles. Good, $40.00; Excellent/Mint, $45.00.

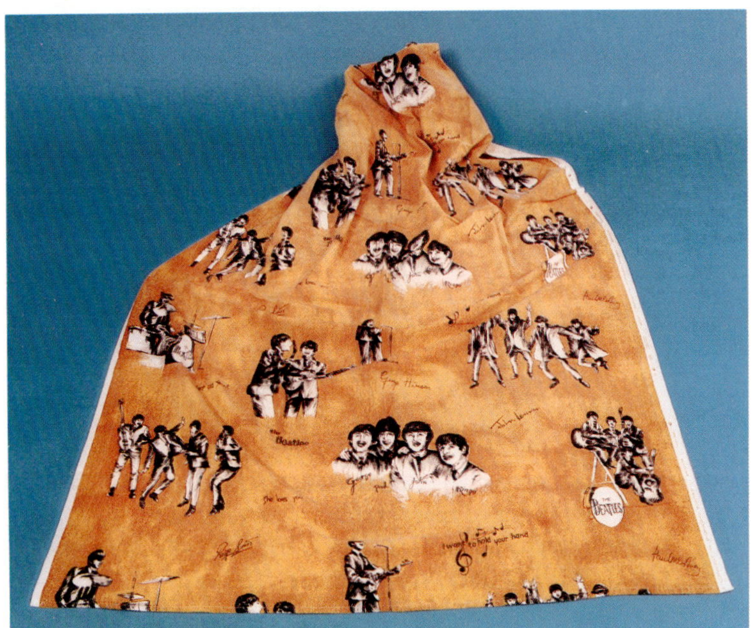

Plate 83. *Curtains* were made in Holland demonstrating that Beatle items were produced in many countries. They are made of cloth. Good, $350.00; Excellent/Mint, $400.00.

Plate 84. *Cup* is an example of a plastic cup distributed in the 1960's. Good, $80.00; Excellent/Mint, $90.00.

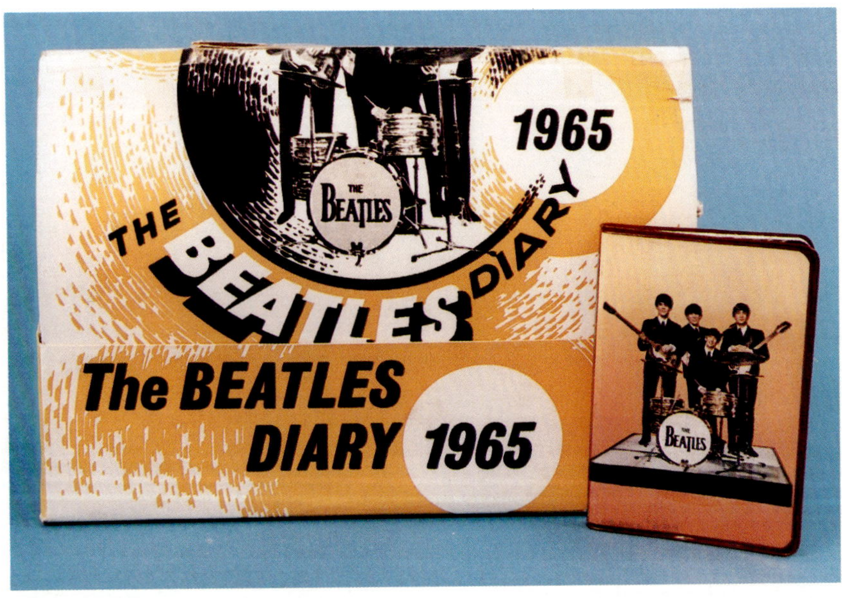

Plate 85. *Diary Display Box* was used as a store display. It was one of the most common store displays. The diary was made in Scotland by the H.B. Longman Company. Good, $200.00; Excellent/Mint, $225.00.

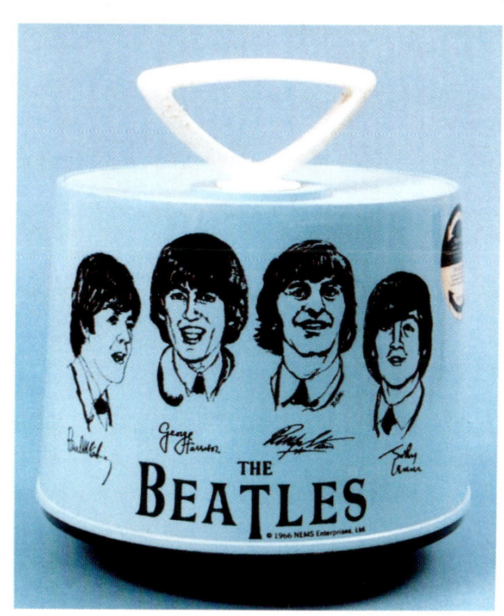

Plate 86. *Disk Go Cases* were made by Charter Industries. They are round and made of plastic. Good, $100.00; Excellent/Mint, $125.00.

Plate 87. *Disk Go Case* in one of the seven color varieties. Good, $100.00; Excellent/Mint, $125.00.

Plate 88. *Disk Go Case* was used to hold 45 records. Good, $100.00; Excellent/Mint, $125.00.

Plate 89. *Disk Go Case*. Good, $100.00; Excellent/Mint, $125.00.

Plate 90. *Disk Go Case*. Good, $100.00; Excellent/Mint, $125.00.

Plate 91. *Disk Go Case*. Good, $100.00; Excellent/Mint, $125.00.

Plate 92. *Dolls* are bobbin' head dolls made by the Carmascot Company and are 8" tall. They are made of composition and the heads bob with use of a spring. Good, $300.00; Excellent/Mint, $350.00.

Plate 93. *Dolls* are of the bobbin' head variety and are in their original box. Good, $500.00; Excellent/Mint, $525.00.

Plate 94. *Dolls* are the display set of bobbin' heads. They are 14" tall and were used in stores to display smaller sets. These are among the most difficult items to find, especially as a complete set. Good, $15,000.00. Excellent/Mint, $18,000.00.

Plate 95. *Doll* 14" John. Good, $3,500.00; Excellent/Mint, $4,000.00.

Plate 97. *Doll* 14" Paul. Good, $3,500.00; Excellent/Mint, $4,000.00.

Plate 96. *Doll* 14" George. Good, $3,500.00; Excellent/Mint, $4,000.00.

Plate 98. *Doll* 14" Ringo. Good, $3,500.00; Excellent/Mint, $4,000.00.

Plate 99. *Dolls* were made by Remco and are in the original boxes. Good, $500.00; Excellent/Mint, $550.00.

Plate 100. *Doll* referred to as the Mascot Doll. It was made by Remco and is 29" tall. It was sold with a cardboard guitar. Good, $200.00; Excellent/Mint, $225.00.

Plate 101. *Dolls* were made by the Remco Company. They are 6½" high and made of plastic. It is important that they have their instruments. Good, $375.00; Excellent/Mint, $400.00.

Plate 102. *Dress* was another product made in Holland. This dress shows the original label. Good, $900.00; Excellent/Mint, $1,100.00.

Plate 103. *Dress* shows the other side with the same pattern in blue. Good, $900.00; Excellent/Mint, $1,100.00.

Plate 104. *Dress* shows the markings inside the dress used to authenticate this product. Good, $900.00; Excellent/Mint, $1,100.00.

Plate 105. *Drawings* produced of all four Beatles and done in detailed line drawings. Good, $70.00; Excellent/Mint, $75.00.

Plate 107. *Drum* was produced by Selcol in England. This style drum has the Ringo signature with a small face of Ringo. It is 14" wide. It is shown with original box and stand. Good, $850.00; Excellent/Mint, $900.00.

Plate 106. *Dress Pattern* was made in Holland and the actual dress was produced from this patterned material. Good, $700.00; Excellent/Mint, $750.00.

Plate 108. *Drum* is another variation of the Ringo drum. It has the large facial picture of Ringo. Good, $650.00; Excellent/Mint, $700.00.

Plate 109. *Drum Box* was produced to hold the New Beat Selcol drum. Good, $200.00; Excellent/Mint, $225.00.

Plate 110. *Drumsticks* were made by Arbiter Ltd. in London. The drumsticks are wooden and are the "Ringo Starr" model. Good, $175.00; Excellent/Mint, $200.00.

Plate 111. *Drum* is the third variation of the Ringo Starr drum by Mastro. It utilizes only the signature on the drum. Good, $800.00; Excellent/Mint, $850.00.

Plate 112. *Drum* is the side view of the New Beat Ringo Drum. Good, $800.00; Excellent/Mint, $850.00.

Plate 113. *Fan* is made of cardboard attached to a wooden stick. Good, $30.00; Excellent/Mint, $35.00.

Plate 114. *Figurines* are made of hard plastic by Subuteo. Good, $120.00; Excellent/Mint, $130.00.

Plate 115. *Fan Club Bulletin* was sent to fan club members. It contained a newsletter and photographs. Good, $40.00; Excellent/Mint, $45.00.

Plate 116. *Flip Your Wig Game* was made by Milton Bradley. It was produced with a colorful game board, 48 cards and four player pieces. Good, $150.00; Excellent/Mint, $175.00.

Plate 117. *Fun Kit* is a magazine which had over 1,000 different things to do inside. It also contained the largest color pin-up ever printed. It was published by Deidre Publications in 1964. Good, $60.00; Excellent/Mint, $65.00.

Plate 118. *Glasses* have the images of Beatles with musical notes on the bottom of each glass. They can be found in a variety of colors. Good, $400.00; Excellent/Mint, $425.00.

Plate 119. *Glasses* were made by J & L Company, Ltd. Each glass has a color decal and a gold rim. This set is 4" in height. Good, $450.00; Excellent/Mint, $475.00.

Plate 120. *Glasses* were produced in only the style of black faces and red notes. They are marked NEMS ENT, Ltd. London. Good, $400.00; Excellent/Mint, $425.00.

Plate 121. *Glass* is referred to as the "Dairy Queen" as it was produced in Canada and used at Dairy Queens. It is the only glass utilizing a star burst. Good, $150.00; Excellent/Mint, $175.00.

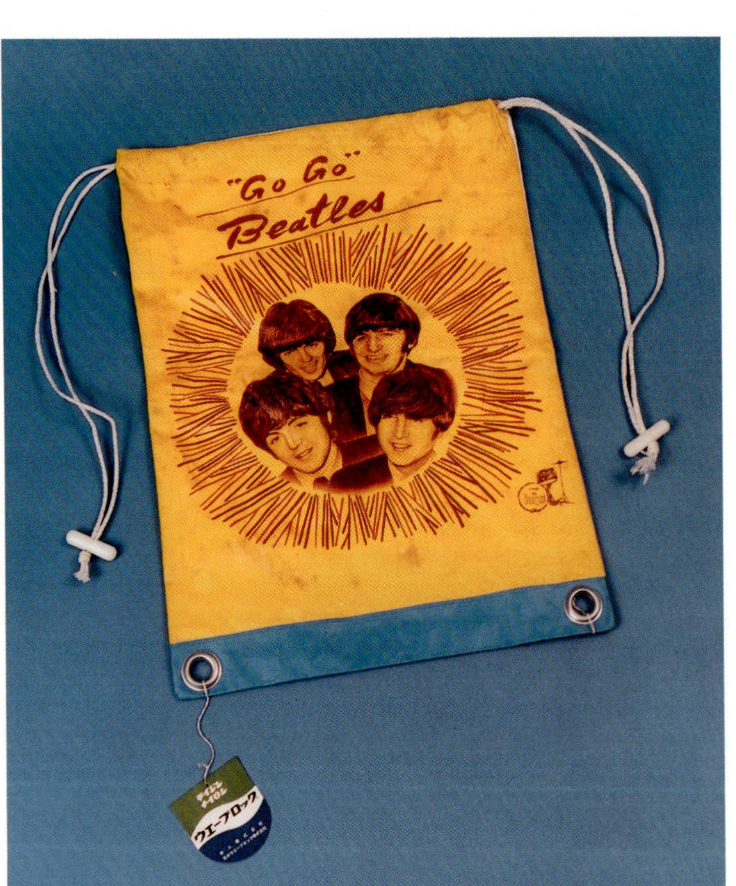

Plate 122. *GoGo Bag* was produced in Japan. It is made of vinyl and is the only one known to exist. Good, $500.00; Excellent/Mint, $550.00.

Plate 123. *Glass* was manufactured in Scotland and pictures the same photo found on diaries. Good, $175.00; Excellent/Mint, $190.00.

Plate 124. *Guitar* (English Version) referred to as a cut away. This guitar is extremely rare. Good, $600.00; Excellent/Mint, $650.00.

Plate 125. *Guitar* (Red Jet) is the only toy electric guitar produced. It was made by Selcol and is 31" tall. Good, $1,200.00; Excellent/Mint, $1,400.00.

Plate 126. *Guitar* (Beatleist) was made by Mastro. It was made with six strings and is 30" tall. Good, $600.00; Excellent/Mint, $650.00.

Plate 127. *Guitar* (Four Pop) made by Mastro is 21" tall. This is the most common guitar. It was manufactured in only red and pink and is totally plastic. Good, $350.00; Excellent/Mint, $400.00.

Plate 128. *Guitar* (JR) was made by Mastro and is only 14¾" making it the smallest of the guitars. Good, $450.00; Excellent/Mint, $500.00.

Plate 129. *Guitar* (Big Six) was made by Selcol and is 33" tall. It came with six strings. Good, $500.00; Excellent/Mint, $550.00.

Plate 130. *Guitar* (New Beat) was made by Selcol and is almost identical to the Big Six except it was made with four strings. It is shown with its original coffin shaped box. Good, $500.00; Excellent/Mint, $550.00.

Plate 131. *Guitar* (New Sound) was made by Selcol. It is 23" tall and was made with four strings. Good, $500.00; Excellent/Mint, $550.00.

Plate 132. *Guitar* is a small guitar used as a jewelry box. Good, $200.00; Excellent/Mint, $225.00.

Plate 133. *Guitar Strings* were made by Hofner and came in a green paper container. Each package contained one guitar string. Good, $150.00; Excellent/Mint, $175.00.

Plate 134. *Gumball Figures* are made of rubber and were placed on a display card. Good, $30.00; Excellent/Mint, $35.00.

Plate 135. *Hairbow* was made by Burlington and it came with two different logo designs. This one is the "I love the Beatle" design. Good, $325.00; Excellent/Mint, $350.00.

Plate 136. *Hairbow* made by Burlington in the signature design. Good, $325.00; Excellent/Mint, $350.00.

Plate 137. *Hairbow* was made by Burlington and this is the very difficult to find red color version. Good, $325.00; Excellent/Mint, $375.00.

Plate 138. *Hairbow* produced in one of the many color variations. Good, $325.00; Excellent/Mint, $350.00.

Plate 139. *Hairbrush* was manufactured by Belliston Products and was produced in a variety of colors. Good, $30.00; Excellent/Mint, $35.00.

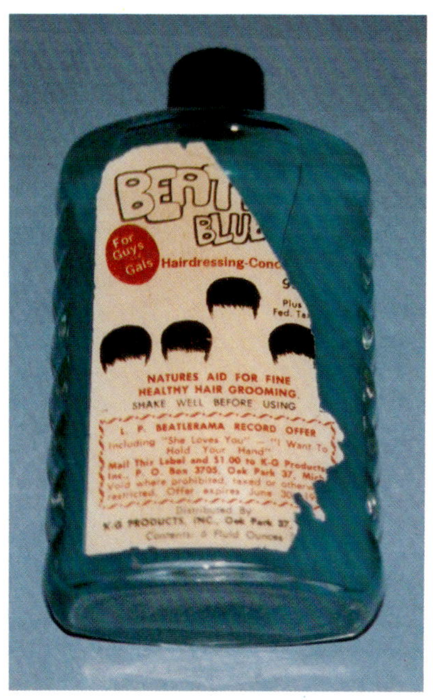

Plate 140. *Hair Dressing* is the only bottle known to exist. It was used as an aid for fine and healthy hair grooming. It was manufactured by K-G Products. Good, $800.00; Excellent/Mint, $850.00

Plate 141. *Hair Spray* was produced by Bronson Products. The can is 8" tall and is a very sought after and hard to find item. Good, $700.00; Excellent/Mint, $725.00.

Plate 142. *Halloween Costume* made by Ben Cooper, a leading maker of Halloween Costumes. It is shown with its original box. Good, $300.00; Excellent/Mint, $325.00.

Plate 143. *Halloween Costume*. Good, $300.00; Excellent/Mint, $325.00.

Plate 144. *Halloween Costume*. Good, $300.00; Excellent/Mint, $325.00.

Plate 145. *Halloween Costume*. Good, $300.00; Excellent/Mint, $325.00.

Plate 146. *Hand Puppet* came only as Ringo and there was one per large display box of candy cigarettes. Good, $235.00; Excellent/Mint, $245.00.

Plate 147. *Handkerchief* is made of cloth and can be found in various colors. Good, $200.00; Excellent/Mint, $215.00.

Plate 148. *Handbag* was produced in a variety of colors and handle configurations. The handles are made of brass. Good, $325.00; Excellent/Mint, $350.00.

Plate 149. *Handbag* is made of vinyl and shows one of the many colors produced. Good, $325.00; Excellent/Mint, $350.00.

Plate 150. *Handbag* is made of vinyl and utilizes portrait and signature design. It has the original tag showing that it sold at Kesslers for $2.00. Good, $325.00; Excellent/Mint, $350.00.

Plate 151. *Handbag* produced in a rare orange color. Good, $325.00; Excellent/Mint, $350.00.

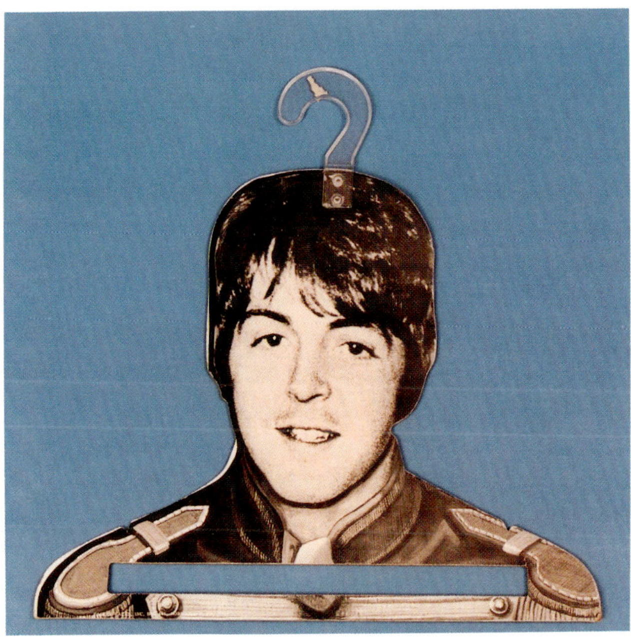

Plate 153. *Hanger*, (Paul). Good, $125.00; Excellent/Mint, $130.00.

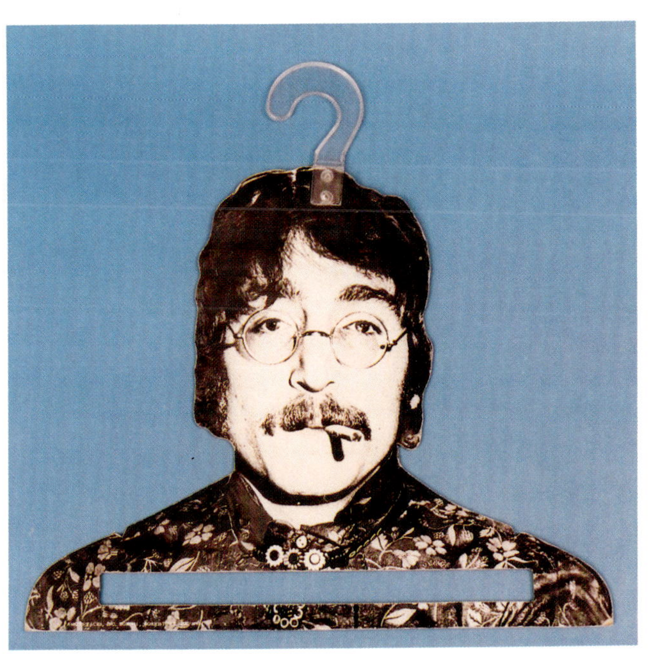

Plate 152. *Hanger* was made by Saunders Ent in England. They are 16" tall and made of cardboard (John). Good, $125.00; Excellent/Mint, $130.00.

Plate 155. *Hanger*, (George). Good, $125.00; Excellent/Mint, $130.00.

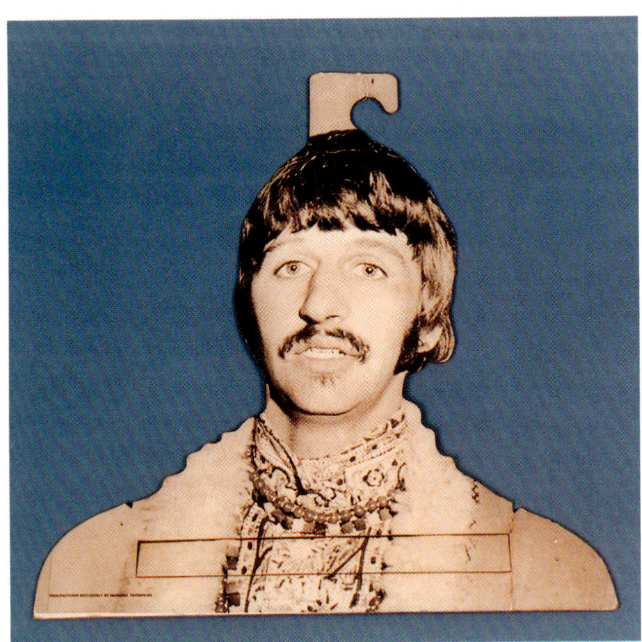

Plate 154. *Hanger*, (Ringo). Good, $125.00; Excellent/Mint, $130.00.

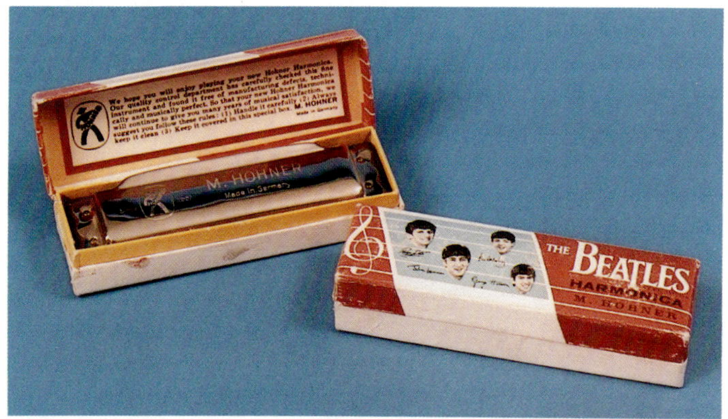

Plate 156. *Harmonica* was made by Hohner and is generic in nature. The box identifies the product as a Beatle piece. Good, $150.00; Excellent/ Mint, $160.00.

Plate 157. *Harmonica Display* opens up into sheet music. Good, $400.00; Excellent/Mint, $425.00.

Plate 158. *Harmonica Display* was made by Hohner and opens to show sheet music. It originally sold for $2.98. Good, $400.00; Excellent/Mint, $425.00.

Plate 159. *Harmonicas* were made in two different boxes. The second box has reversed the signatures with faces of George and Paul. Good, $125.00; Excellent/Mint, $135.00.

Plate 160. *Hat* is referred to as a beach hat. It was produced in different colors. Good, $120.00; Excellent/Mint, $130.00.

Plate 161. *Hat* is another beach hat color variation. Good, $120.00; Excellent/Mint, $130.00.

Plate 162. *Hatbox* is made of vinyl by AirFlite. They were manufactured in only two colors — black and red. Good, $550.00; Excellent/Mint, $575.00.

Plate 163. *Hatbox* is the other color variation of the AirFlite product. Good, $550.00; Excellent/Mint, $575.00.

Plate 164. *Headband* was made by Better Wear, Inc., and can be found in a variety of eight colors. Good, $50.00; Excellent/Mint, $60.00.

Plate 165. *Headband* is an Australian product made by LTC Vincent. It is a rare headband. Good, $250.00; Excellent/Mint, $275.00.

Plate 166. *Headband* is an unusual variation using faces and signature design. Good, $170.00; Excellent/Mint, $180.00.

Plate 167. *Headband* was produced by Burlington and is made of cloth. Good, $125.00; Excellent/Mint, $150.00.

Plate 168. *Headphones* are an incredible item produced by Koss Electronics who still produce headphones today. The Beatle phones have a sticker on each earphone. A boxed set is very difficult to find. Good, $1,800.00; Excellent/Mint, $2,000.00.

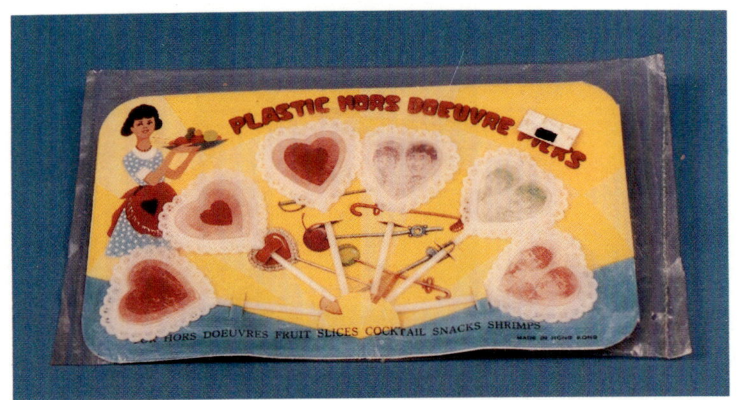

Plate 169. *Hors D'oeuvre Picks* were made in Hong Kong and flash between Beatles and hearts. Good, $115.00; Excellent/Mint, $120.00.

Plate 170. *Ice Cream Wrapper* used for the Hood ice cream bar. This is one of the more common paper variety. Good, $20.00; Excellent/Mint, $25.00.

Plate 171. *Hummer and Hummer Box* were produced by Louis F. Dow Company. The hummer is a musical instrument made of cardboard. All of them were produced with this pattern. Good, $250.00; Excellent/Mint, $300.00.

Plate 172. *Inflatables* are made of plastic and when blown up measure 13" tall. Good, $115.00; Excellent/Mint, $135.00.

Plate 173. *Inflatables* shown in their original packaging. Good, $150.00; Excellent/Mint, $160.00.

Plate 175. *Inflatable Advertisement* shown on the front of a Lux soap box. The box was available in a variety of colors. Good, $400.00; Excellent/Mint, $425.00.

Plate 174. *Inflatable Advertisement* shown on a Lux soap box. Good, $400.00; Excellent/Mint, $425.00.

Photo 176. *Iron Transfer* used on items of clothing. Good, $35.00; Excellent/Mint, $40.00.

Photo 177. *Kaboodle Kit* was manufactured by Standard Plastic Production, Inc. They were available in a variety of colors. One of the most desired Beatle collectibles. Good, $850.00; Excellent/Mint, $900.00.

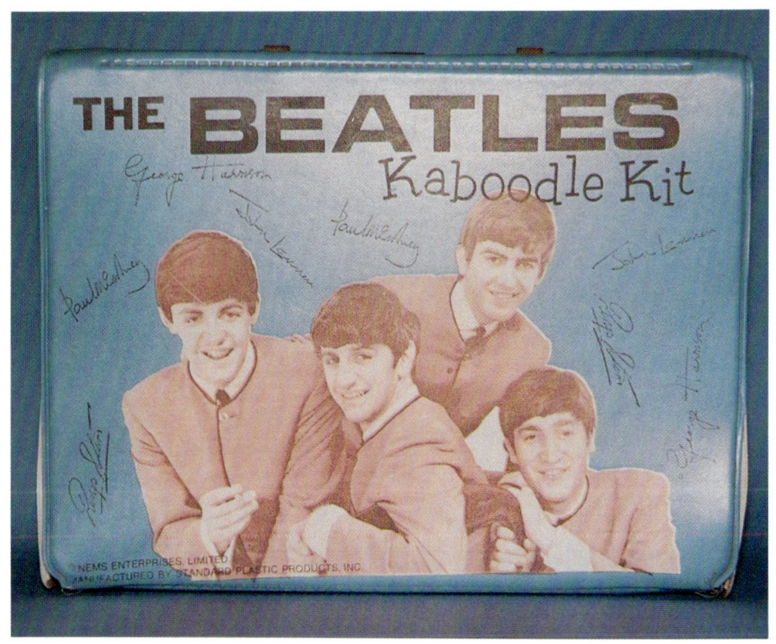

Plate 178. *Kaboodle Kit* produced in another of the color varieties. Good, $850.00; Excellent/Mint, $925.00.

Plate 179. *Lamp* was hung by a screw to the wall. The shade is paper and came without a bulb holder. Good, $600.00; Excellent/Mint, $650.00.

Plate 180. *Lamp* is a paper cylinder with wire legs so that it stands. Inside is a place for a light bulb. Good, $700.00; Excellent/Mint, $725.00.

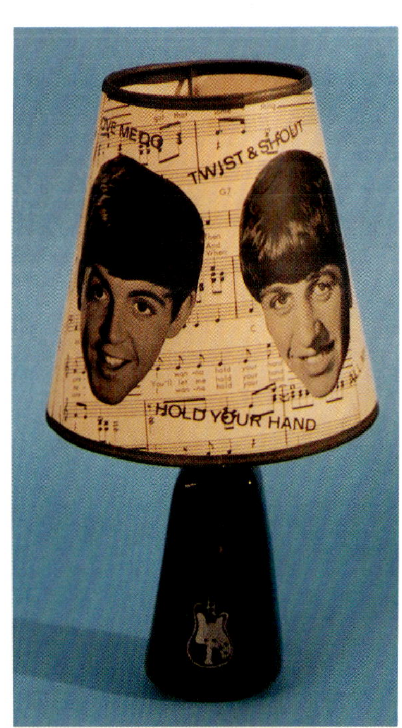

Plate 181. *Lamp* is the rarest of the three types produced. The shade is cardboard and the base is ceramic with a gold guitar painted on it. Good, $1,100.00; Excellent/Mint, $1,200.00.

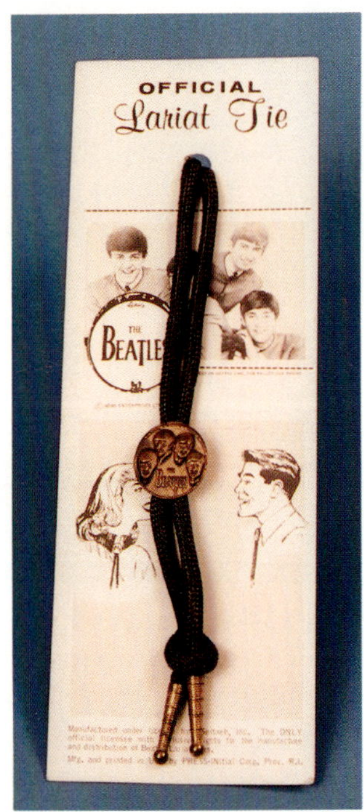

Plate 182. *Lariat Tie* was made by the Press Initial Corporation. The disk is made of brass. Good, $200.00; Excellent/Mint, $225.00.

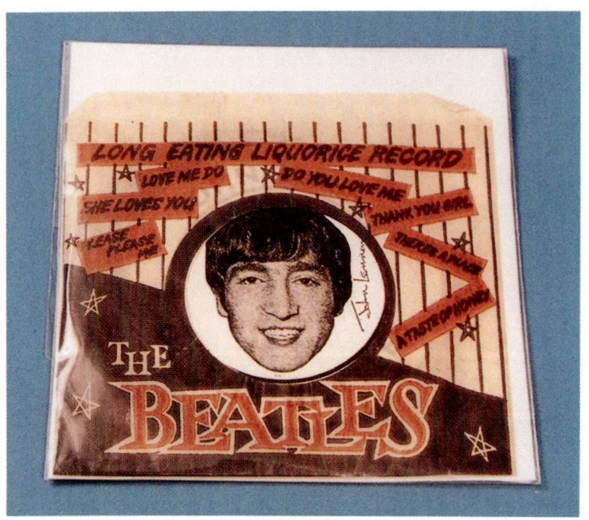

Plate 183. *Licorice Candy Record* (John) was made by Clevedon Confectionery. Good, $200.00; Excellent/Mint, $225.00.

Plate 184. *Licorice Candy Record* (George) is hard to find with original licorice record inside. Good, $200.00; Excellent/Mint, $225.00.

Plate 185. *Licorice Candy Record* (Ringo) was made with a paper sleeve. Good, $200.00; Excellent/Mint, $225.00.

Photo 187. *Litter Holder* is vinyl and made by AirFlite. It opens up and could be used in a car for litter. Good, $300.00; Excellent/Mint, $325.00.

Photo 186. *Linen* was made by Ulster and is referred to as Irish Linen. It is used as a wall hanging. Good, $175.00; Excellent/Mint, $200.00.

Photo 189. *Magnetic Hairstyle Game* was produced by Merit. It is made of heavy cardboard and utilizes magnets. Good, $500.00; Excellent/Mint, $525.00.

Photo 188. *Lunch Box* was produced by Aladdin Industries. It is made of metal and comes with the appropriate blue thermos. It is very sought after by lunch box collectors. Good, $300.00; Excellent/Mint, $350.00.

Photo 190. *Marionette* (George) is made of wood and the maker is unknown. These individual marionettes are very rare. Good, $400.00; Excellent/Mint, $425.00.

Photo 191. *Marionette* (Ringo). Good, $400.00; Excellent/Mint, $425.00.

Photo 192. *Marionette* (John). Good, $400.00; Excellent/Mint, $425.00.

Plate 193. *Model* (Ringo) was made by the Revell Company, maker of many types of models. Good, $250.00; Excellent/Mint, $275.00.

Plate 194. *Model* (George) is greater in price when package is sealed and unopened. Good, $250.00; Excellent/Mint, $275.00.

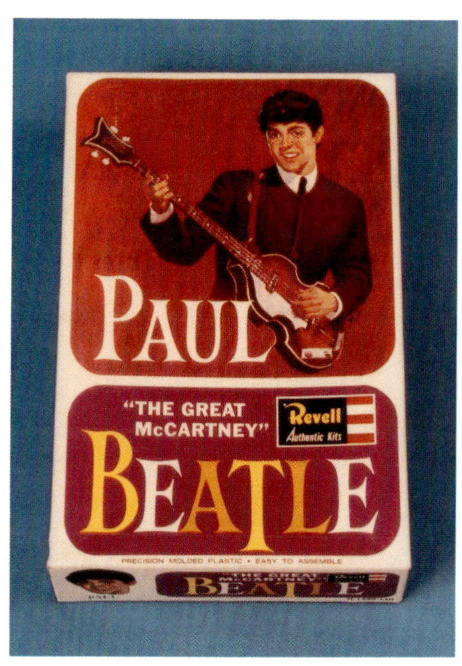

Plate 195. *Model* (Paul). Good, $250.00; Excellent/Mint, $275.00.

Plate 196. *Model* (John). Good, $250.00; Excellent/Mint, $275.00.

Plate 198. *Mug* was produced in Canada and is made of pottery. Good, $150.00; Excellent/Mint, $160.00.

Plate 197. *Movie* is silent, 8mm and shows highlights from their US visit. The card is very hard to find. It is a silent movie of *A Hard Day's Night*. Good, $800.00; Excellent/Mint, $825.00.

Plate 199. *Mug* is another variation of the Canadian product. Good, $150.00; Excellent/Mint, $160.00.

Plate 200. *Napkins* are found in their original packaging. There are a total of 50 napkins included. Good, $700.00; Excellent/Mint, $725.00.

Plate 201. *Napkin* shows the individual product when opened up. Good, $35.00; Excellent/Mint, $40.00.

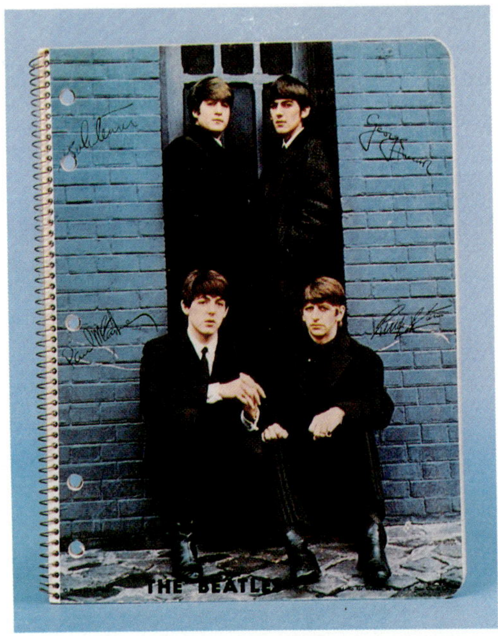

Plate 202. *Notebooks* (group) were made by Westab. This is an example of one that is spiral bound. Good, $100.00; Excellent/Mint, $125.00.

Plate 203. *Notebook* (group) was produced by Westab. It measures 8½" x 11". This example has the binding on the side. Good, $100.00; Excellent/Mint, $125.00.

Plate 204. *Notebook* (group) shows an example of one bound at the top. Good, $100.00; Excellent/Mint, $125.00.

Plate 205. *Notebook* (group) shows another variation with three holes. Good, $100.00; Excellent/Mint, $125.00.

Plate 207. *Nylons* made by Ballito shown from the back side with the Beatles' pictures and signatures. Good, $130.00; Excellent/Mint, $140.00.

Plate 206. *Nylons* were made by Scott-Centenaire Company. This is an example of the Ballito textured mesh stockings. Good, $130.00; Excellent/Mint, $140.00.

Plate 208. *Nylons* referred to as carefree. Good, $150.00; Excellent/Mint, $160.00.

Plate 210. *Nylons Display Card* used to promote Ballito stockings in conjunction with the Movie *A Hard Day's Night*. Good, $400.00; Excellent/Mint, $425.00.

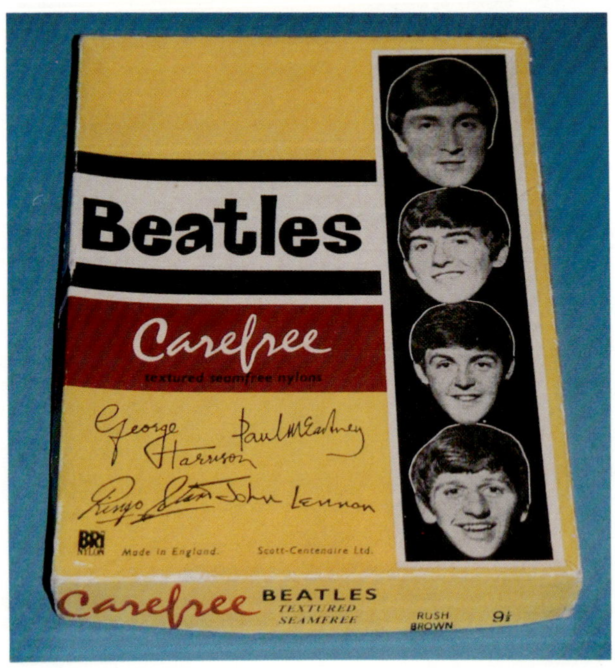

Plate 209. *Nylon Box* held several pairs of the carefree variety of nylons. Good, $350.00; Excellent/Mint, $400.00.

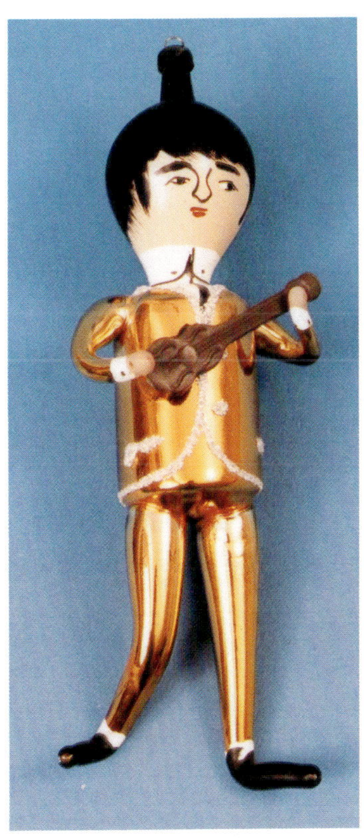

Plate 211. *Ornaments* were used to hang on Christmas trees. Each was hand blown, so they may vary. Good, $300.00; Excellent/Mint, $325.00.

Plate 213. *Ornaments* were produced in a variety of colors like the blue one pictured here. Good, $300.00; Excellent/Mint, $325.00.

Plate 212. *Ornaments* have the guitar in either left or right hand and that identifies which Beatle it is. Good, $300.00; Excellent/Mint, $325.00.

Plate 214. *Oil Painting* was made by Beatles Buddies for Fan Club usage. They were sold in a set of four, one of each Beatle. Good, $70.00; Excellent/Mint, $75.00.

Plate 215. *Paint by Number* was produced by Artistic Creations. Good, $1,200.00; Excellent/Mint, $1,300.00.

Plate 216. *Paint by Number* included paints, brush and one Beatle portrait to paint. Good, $1,200.00; Excellent/Mint, $1,300.00.

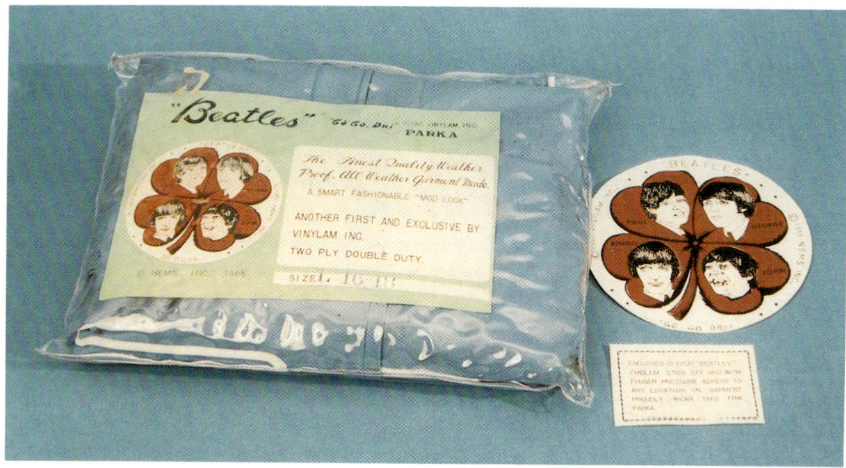

Plate 217. *Beatles Parka* is the only one known to exist and it is marked 1985 NEMS. It was made by Vinyl Lamb, Inc., and is referred to as GoGo Dri Parka. Good, $900.00; Excellent/Mint, $1,000.00.

Plate 218. *Pens* were made by the Press Initial Corporation. They were produced in many colors but all feature four heads on the pen top. Good, $120.00; Excellent/Mint, $130.00.

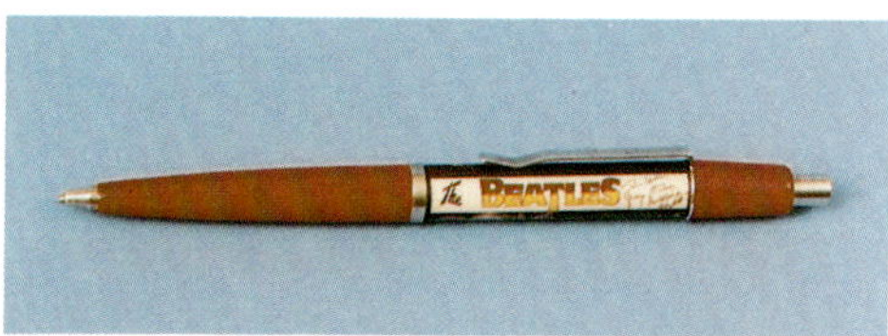

Plate 219. *Pen* was made in Denmark and is very hard to find. It is plastic. Good, $120.00; Excellent/Mint, $130.00.

Plate 220. *Pen*. Good, $120.00; Excellent/Mint, $130.00.

Plate 221. *Pencil Cases* were by Standard Plastic Products and are made of vinyl. Good, $140.00; Excellent/Mint, $145.00.

Plate 222. *Pencil Case* in another color variety of this product. Good, $140.00; Excellent/Mint, $145.00.

Plate 223. *Pencil Cases*. This is the gray version. It is copyrighted Raymat & Company. Good, $140.00; Excellent/Mint, $145.00.

Plate 224. *Pencil Pouch* red. Good, $150.00; Excellent/Mint, $175.00.

Plate 225. *Pencil Pouch* turquoise. Good, $150.00; Excellent/Mint, $175.00.

Plate 226. *Pennant*. Good, $85.00; Excellent/Mint, $90.00.

Plate 228. *Pennant* was made by Irwin Specialities. It is 22" long. Good, $100.00; Excellent/Mint, $125.00.

Plate 227. *Pennant*. Good, $35.00; Excellent/Mint, $40.00.

Plate 229. *Pennant*. Good, $20.00; Excellent/Mint, $25.00.

Plate 230. *Pennant*. Good, $60.00; Excellent/Mint, $65.00.

Plate 231. *Pennant*. Good, $50.00; Excellent/Mint, $60.00.

Plate 232. *Pennant*. Good, $60.00; Excellent/Mint, $65.00.

Plate 233. *Pennant*. Good, $35.00; Excellent/Mint, $40.00.

Plate 234. *Pennant*. Good, $70.00; Excellent/Mint, $75.00.

Plate 235. *Pillow* was made by Nordic House and is 12". This variety is the rarest. Good, $200.00; Excellent/Mint, $225.00.

Plate 236. *Pillow* is another variety produced by Nordic House. Good, $125.00; Excellent/Mint, $150.00.

Plate 237. *Pillow* is the only one of this rare variation known to exist. The strap is not known to have ever existed. This pillow was sold only at California concerts. Good, $325.00; Excellent/Mint, $350.00.

Plate 238. *Pillow* is the most common showing the Beatles from the waist up. Good, $175.00; Excellent/Mint, $200.00.

Plate 240. *Placemats* are made of canvas. Good, $60.00; Excellent/Mint, $65.00.

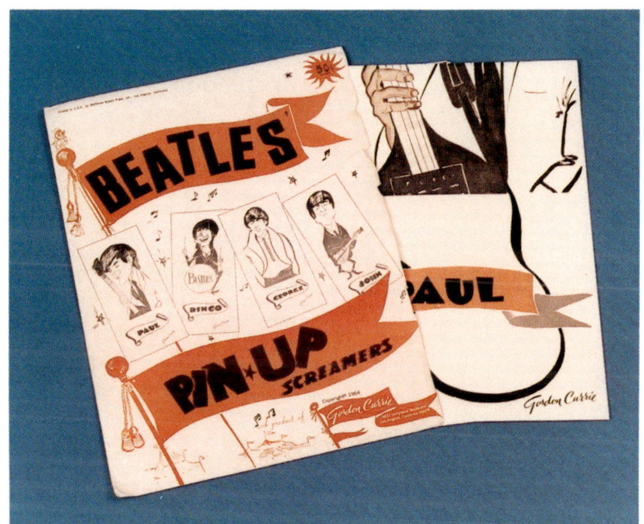

Plate 239. *Pin-up Screamers* were made by Matthews Rotary Press. There is one drawing of each Beatle. Good, $90.00; Excellent/Mint, $100.00.

Plate 241. *Placards* came in a set of different Beatles sayings. Good, $15.00; Excellent/Mint, $20.00.

Plate 242. *Pomade* was made by H. H. Cosmetic Lab in the Philippines. The box held fifty of the small packets of hair grease. They sold originally for 10 cents each. Good, $3,200.00; Excellent/Mint, $3,500.00.

Plate 243. *Playing Cards* can be found in two box varieties both pictured here. Good, $275.00; Excellent/Mint, $325.00.

Plate 244. *Postcards* show a variety of sizes and images produced. Good, $20.00; Excellent/Mint, $25.00.

Plate 245. *Portraits* (Ringo Starr) were suitable for framing. Good, $100.00; Excellent/Mint, $110.00.

Plate 246. *Portraits* (Paul). Good, $100.00; Excellent/Mint, $110.00.

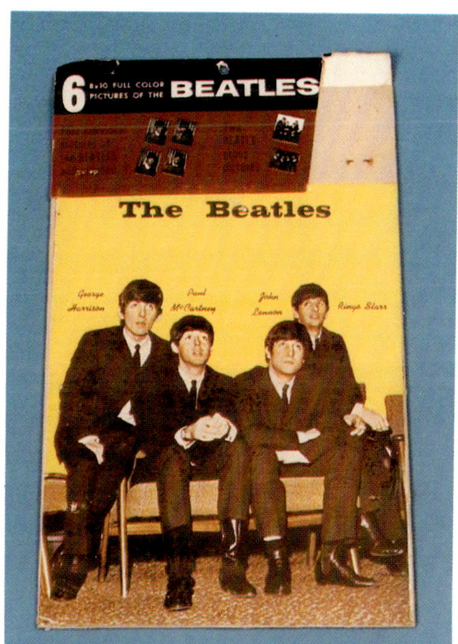

Plate 247. *Portraits* included six 8" x 10 " pictures of the Beatles and were made by J.M. Distributors. Good, $115.00; Excellent/Mint, $120.00.

Plate 248. *Portraits* were done on paper by Volpe. Good, $120.00; Excellent/Mint, $130.00.

Plate 249. *Poster* was made by Dell and is 54" x 20". Good, $75.00; Excellent/Mint, $100.00.

Plate 250. *Poster* was made by Dell and is shown here in the original packaging. Good, $50.00; Excellent/Mint, $60.00.

Plate 251. *Poster* was made by Dell and sold for 25 cents. Good, $50.00; Excellent/Mint, $60.00.

Plate 252. *Poster* is one of the largest made and is shown here in original mailer. It was made by PYX Products. Good, $80.00; Excellent/Mint, $90.00.

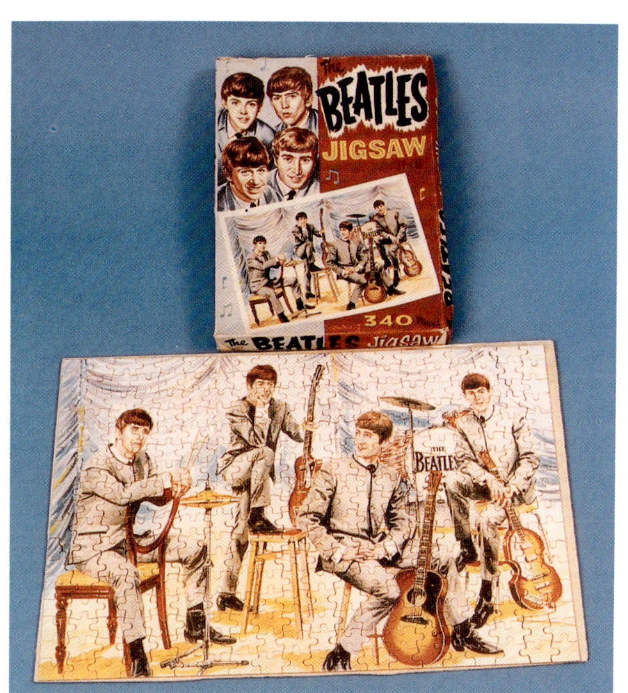

Plate 253. *Puzzle* is of the jigsaw variety. When completed, it measures 17" x 11" and utilizes 340 pieces. Good, $300.00; Excellent/Mint, $350.00.

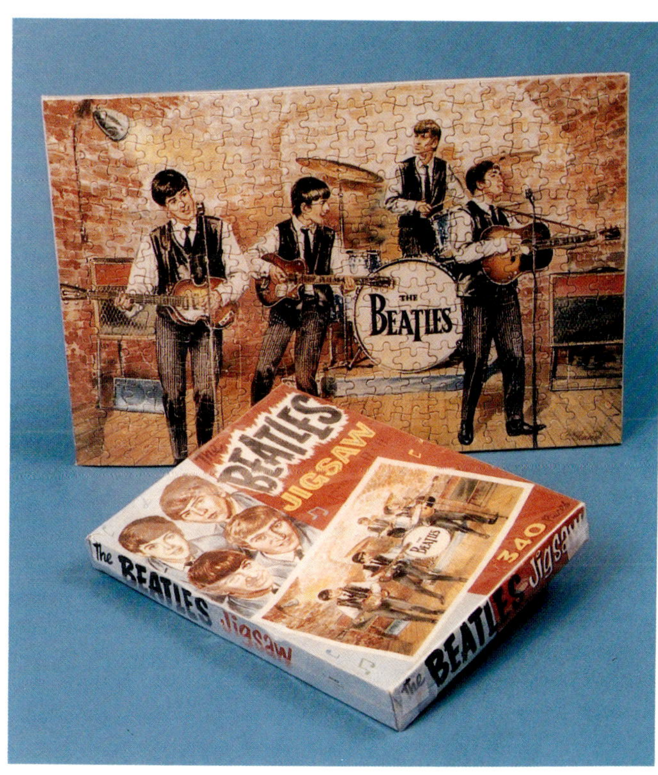

Plate 254. *Puzzle* is of the jigsaw variety and utilizes 340 pieces. Good, $300.00; Excellent/Mint, $350.00.

Plate 255. *Puzzle* is referred to as the "Illustrated Lyrics Puzzle." Hidden in the puzzle can be found thirteen Beatle song titles. There are a total of 800 pieces. Good, $300.00; Excellent/Mint, $350.00.

Plate 256. *Record Carrier* was produced by Seagull Enterprises. It can hold 45 records and utilizes plastic sleeves for the records. Good, $200.00; Excellent/Mint, $225.00.

Plate 257. *Record Case* was made by AirFlite and is heavy cardboard. This model was designed to hold 33 rpm records. Good, $200.00; Excellent/Mint, $225.00.

Plate 258. *Record Player* is four-speed and has the picture of the Beatles in top half. Good, $1,500.00; Excellent/Mint, $1,800.00.

Plate 259. *Record Player* was produced in a limited quantity. The front has a Beatles sticker on the right side. Good, $1,500.00; Excellent/Mint, $1,800.00.

Plate 260. *Rug* was produced in Belgium and measures 33¼" x 2¼". Good, $400.00; Excellent/Mint, $425.00.

Plate 261. *Scarf* is the original package with original tag. It was made by Scammonden Woolen Company in England. Good, $350.00; Excellent/Mint, $375.00.

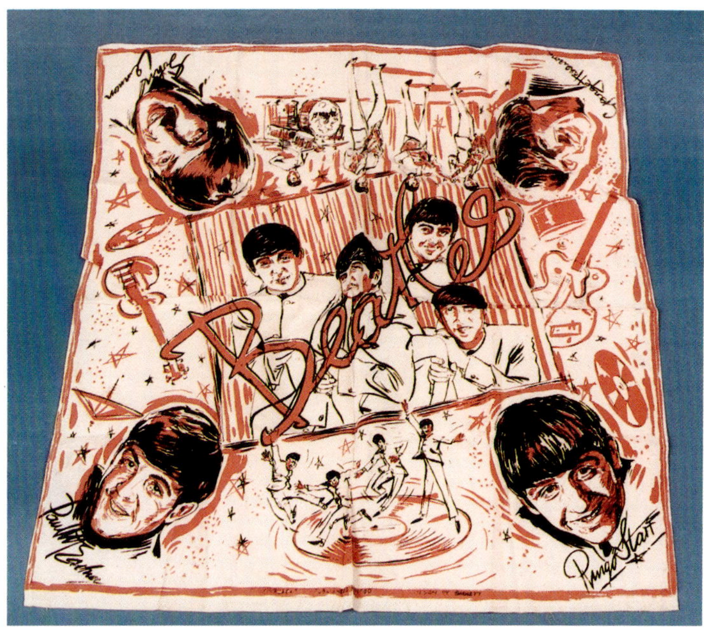

Plate 262. *Scarf* was made by Blackpool Publishers. It is 26 inches. Good, $170.00; Excellent/Mint, $175.00.

Plate 263. *Scarf* is shown with original tag. It measures 26". Good, $140.00; Excellent/Mint, $145.00.

Plate 264. *Scarf* is the same as plate 262 but has fringe along the edge. Good, $140.00; Excellent/Mint, $145.00.

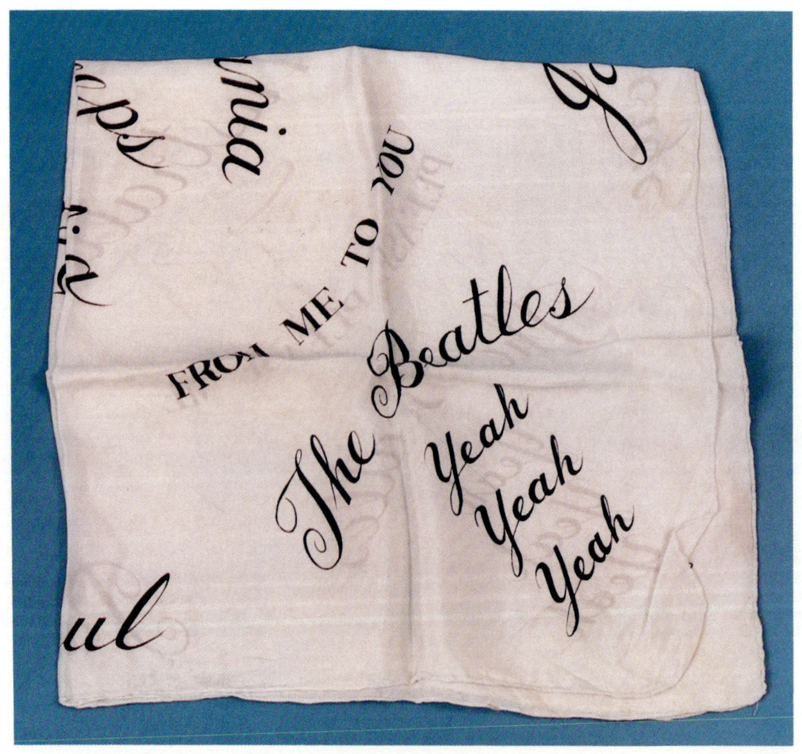

Plate 265. *Scarf* is a very rare one that was produced in Australia. Good, $200.00; Excellent/Mint, $220.00.

Plate 266. *Scarf* thought to be produced in England. It is made of cloth with leatherette straps. Good, $100.00; Excellent/Mint, $115.00.

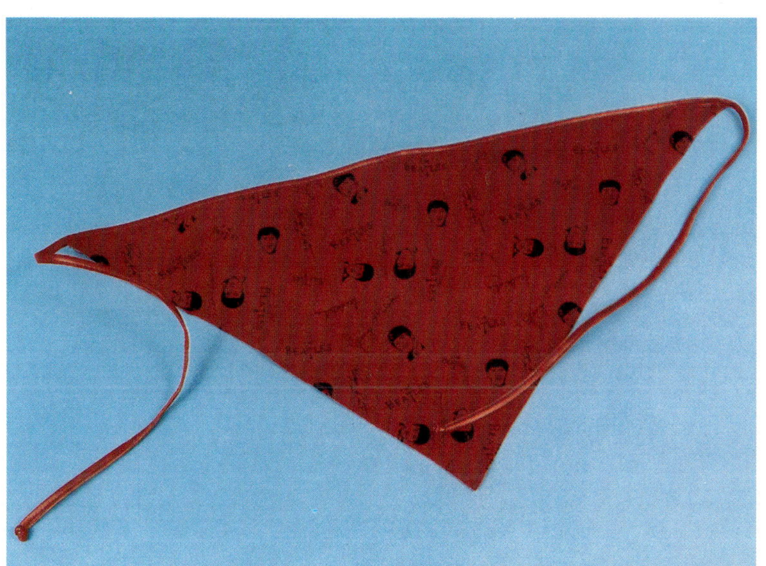

Plate 267. *Scarf* is the solid red version of the triangular scarf. Good, $100.00; Excellent/Mint, $115.00.

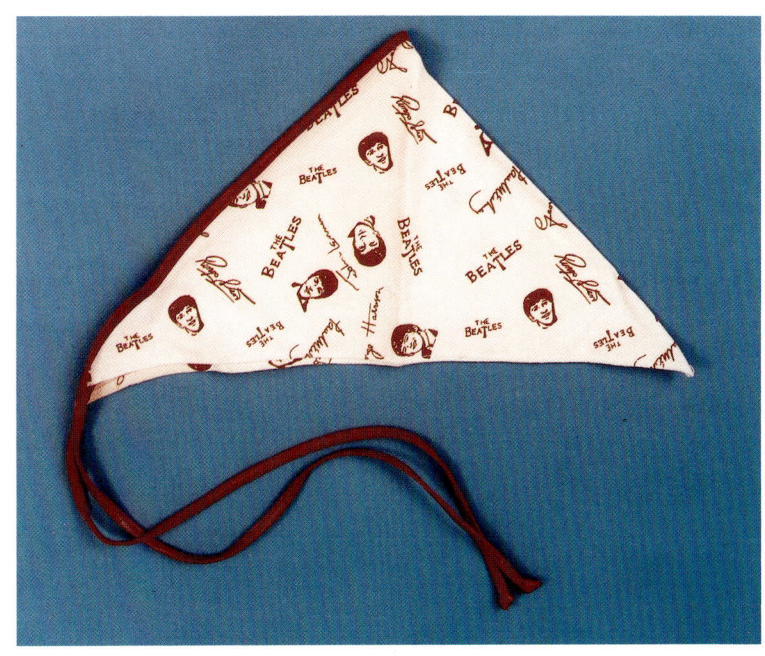

Plate 268. *Scarf* is another variation of the English triangular scarf. Good, $100.00; Excellent/Mint, $115.00.

Plate 269. *School Report Cover* was produced by Select-O-Pak. It can be found in a variety of colors. Good, $120.00; Excellent/Mint, $125.00.

Plate 270. *Scrap Book* was made by Whitman. It originally cost 29 cents. Good, $85.00; Excellent/Mint, $95.00.

Plate 271. *Shirt* is of the knit variety. The label inside states "The only Authentic Beatle shirt." Good, $170.00; Excellent/Mint, $180.00.

Plate 272. *Shoulder Bag* is made of vinyl with a rope or cord as a strap. This version is the rarest and thought to be Canadian. Good, $400.00; Excellent/Mint, $425.00.

Plate 273. *Shoulder Bag* is made of vinyl. Good, $475.00; Excellent/Mint, $500.00.

Plate 274. *Shoulder Bag* is 9½" x 10". This is a rare pink color variation. Good, $400.00; Excellent/Mint, $425.00.

Plate 275. *Splatter Toy* was made by Splatter Toy Company. Included with the toy were instructions. Good, $300.00; Excellent/Mint, $350.00.

Plate 276. *Stamps* were made by Hallmark. There were 100 stamps included. The stamps are one sheet of each Beatle and one page of a group shot. Good, $50.00; Excellent/Mint, $65.00.

Plate 277. *Stamp Store Display* for the Hallmark set. Good, $250.00; Excellent/Mint, $275.00.

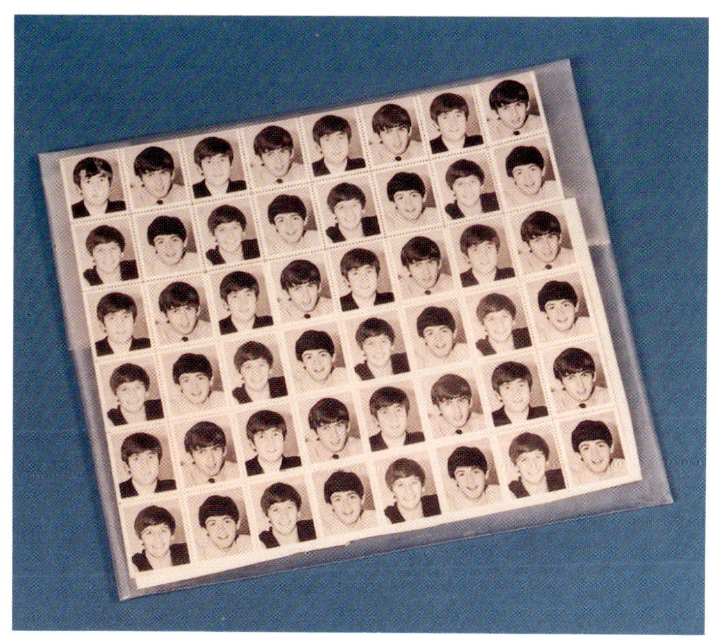

Plate 278. *Stamps* were sold in a sheet of 48 black and white stamps. Good, $50.00; Excellent/Mint, $60.00.

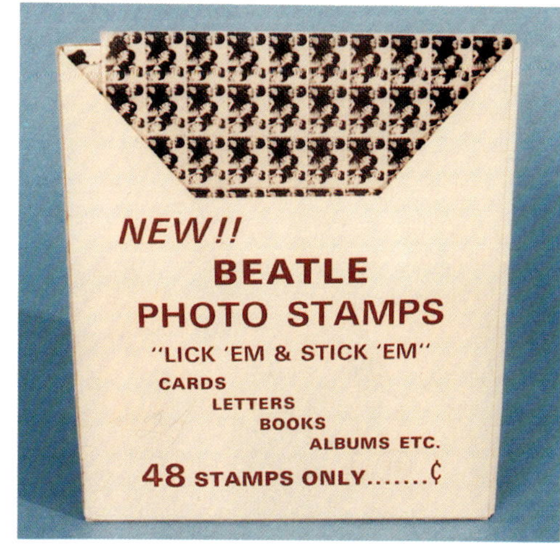

Plate 279. *Stamps Store Display*. Good, $270.00; Excellent/Mint, $285.00.

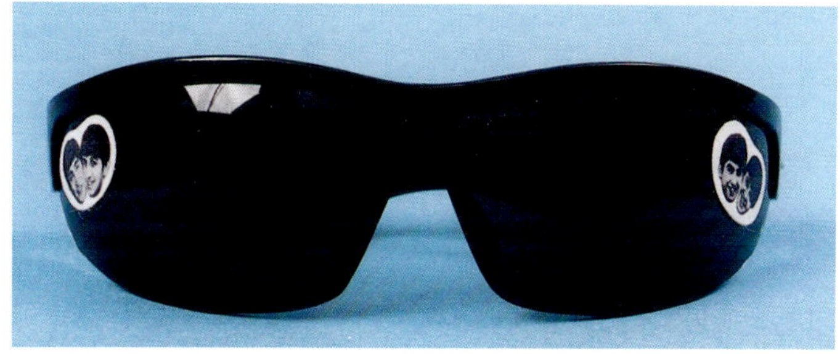

Plate 280. *Sunglasses* were made by Solarex. It is essential that the two stickers be in place. Good, $235.00; Excellent/Mint, $255.00.

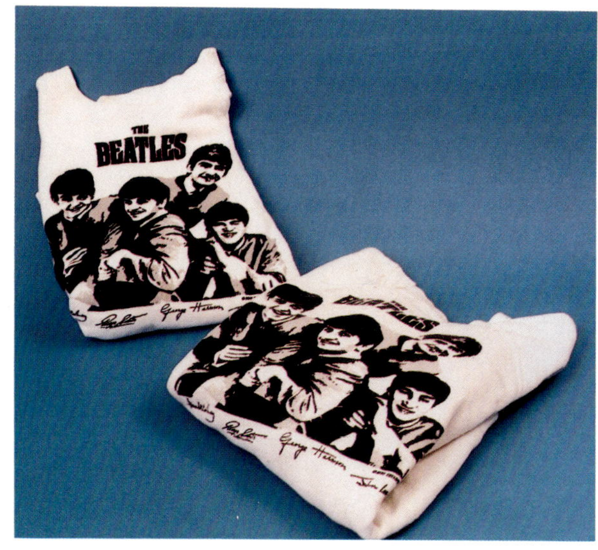

Plate 281. *Sweatshirts* are made of cotton and have no clothing tags. They are long sleeved. Good, $150.00; Excellent/Mint, $160.00.

Plate 282. *Swingers Music Set*. Good, $150.00; Excellent/Mint, $175.00.

Plate 283. *Swingers Music Set*. Good, $60.00; Excellent/Mint, $70.00.

Plate 284. *Swingers Music Set*. Good, $100.00; Excellent/Mint, $125.00.

Plate 285. *Tablecloth* is made of vinyl and utilized a continuous pattern. Good, $300.00; Excellent/Mint, $325.00.

Plate 286. *Talc* was made by Margo of Mayfair. It is 7" tall. Good, $500.00; Excellent/Mint, $550.00.

Plate 287. *Tennis Shoes* were manufactured by Wing Dings. This is the low cut variety. Good, $450.00; Excellent/Mint, $500.00.

Plate 288. *Tennis Shoes* are the rarer blue variety produced by Wing Dings. Good, $500.00; Excellent/Mint, $550.00.

Plate 289. *Tennis Shoes* are the rarest high top variety. They were also made by Wing Ding. Good, $700.00; Excellent/Mint, $725.00.

Plate 290. *Ticket* was used for a Kansas City concert presented by Charles O. Finley. Good, $50.00; Excellent/Mint, $65.00.

Plate 291. *Tile* is the most difficult to find showing all the Beatles. Good, $250.00; Excellent/Mint, $275.00.

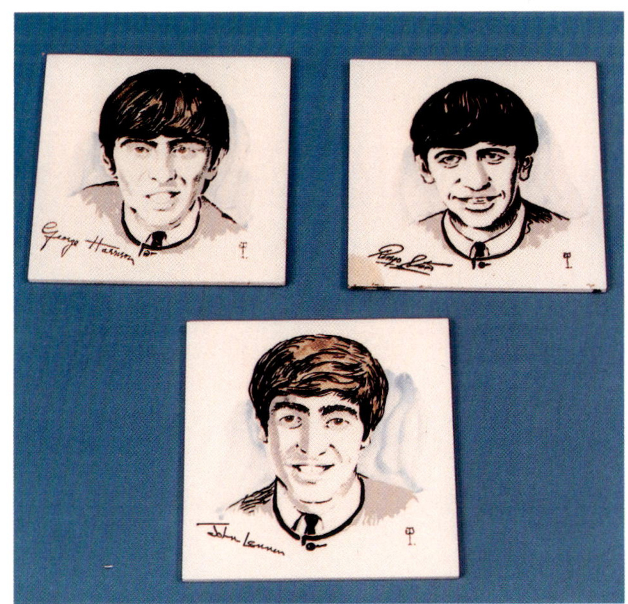

Plate 292. *Tiles.* They are each 6" x 6" and ceramic. They are marked on the back. Good, $200.00; Excellent/Mint, $225.00.

Plate 293. *Trading Cards* (Color Photo Box) contained 24 packs of colorized trading cards. Good, $700.00; Excellent/Mint, $725.00.

Plate 295. *Trading Cards* (Color Series Rack Pack) contained three packs of ten cards each. Header card is essential. Good, $160.00; Excellent/Mint, $170.00.

Plate 294. *Trading Cards* (*A Hard Day's Night* Movie Box) contained twenty four packs of black and white cards with scenes from the movie. Good, $650.00; Excellent/Mint, $675.00.

Plate 296. *Trading Cards* (New Series) held twenty four packs of new series cards. Box top flips for use in stores. Good, $700.00; Excellent/Mint, $725.00.

Plate 297. *Trading Cards* (*A Hard Day's Night* Pack) contained five trading cards. Good, $45.00; Excellent/Mint, $50.00.

Plate 298. *Trading Cards* (Black and White Series Wrapper) made by the A & BC Company and contained black and white autographed cards. Good, $100.00; Excellent/Mint, $110.00.

Plate 299. *Trays* were made by Worcester Ware. There was a reproduction so the label on the back authenticates the piece. Good, $40.00; Excellent/Mint, $60.00.

Plate 300. *Tumbler* is 6¼" and made of plastic. Good, $120.00; Excellent/Mint, $130.00.

Plate 301. *Tumbler Insert* is made of paper and fits into tumbler. Good, $20.00; Excellent/Mint, $25.00.

Plate 302. *Twig* is a toy made in Spartanburg, South Carolina. It contained two wooden dowels and two plastic spinners. Good, $300.00; Excellent/Mint, $350.00.

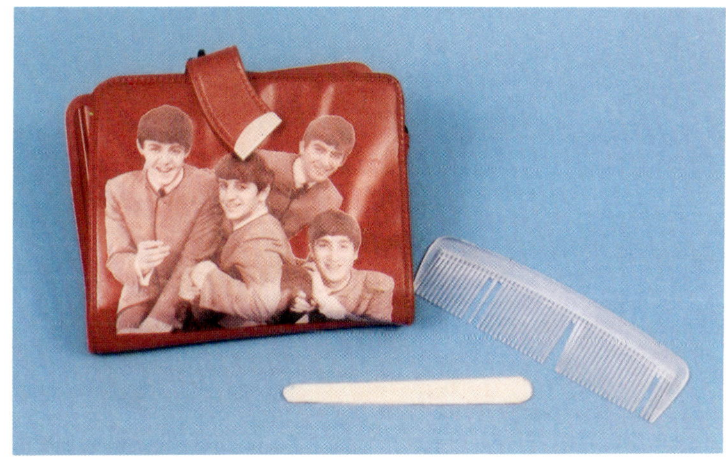

Photo 303. *Wallet* was made by Standard Plastic Products. Sold with the wallet was a nail file and a comb. Good, $130.00; Excellent/Mint, $135.00.

Photo 304. *Wallet* shown in its original packaging. This wallet came with key holder, change purse, mirror, comb, picture holder and emery board. Good, $400.00; Excellent/Mint, $425.00.

Plate 305. *Wallet* is another type that was sold. Good, $150.00; Excellent/Mint, $175.00.

Plate 306. *Wallet Dollars* were placed in these plastic holders for use in gumball machines. Good, $30.00; Excellent/Mint, $35.00.

Plate 307. *Wallet* in the very hard to find black variation. Good, $200.00; Excellent/Mint, $225.00.

Plate 308. *Wallet Dollar Display* went on or in the gumball machine. Good, $60.00; Excellent/Mint, $65.00.

Plate 309. *Wallet Photos* were made by Dell and included biographies and horoscopes. Good, $60.00; Excellent/Mint, $65.00.

Plate 310. *Wallpaper* was sold in rolls measuring 21" x 21". This is a piece of one of the panels. Good, $225.00; Excellent/Mint, $250.00.

Plate 311. *Wig* was made by Lowell Toy Manufacturing Corporation. Good, $95.00; Excellent/Mint, $105.00.

CHAPTER TWO

Jewelry

The number of different Beatle jewelry pieces produced is incredible. Most came on their own display cards which increase the values substantially. In many cases the display cards were done in both black and white and color variations.

Unknown jewelry pieces are turning up in the marketplace constantly. It is apparent that variations of many of the pieces were made in different countries.

Plate 312. *Brooch Watch* was made by Smiths. It is the only one known to exist. Good, $2,200.00; Excellent/Mint, $2,500.00.

Plate 313. *Tie Tac*. Good, $95.00; Excellent/Mint, $100.00. *Key Chain*. Good, $100.00; Excellent/Mint, $105.00. *Brooch*, Good, $120.00; Excellent/Mint, $125.00. *Ring*, Good, $85.00; Excellent/Mint, $90.00. *Necklace*. Good, $120.00; Excellent/Mint, $125.00.

Plate 314. *Cuff Links*. Good, $150.00; Excellent/Mint, $160.00. *Tie Clip*. Good, $150.00; Excellent/Mint, $160.00. *Beatles Pin*. Good, $150.00; Excellent/Mint, $160.00.

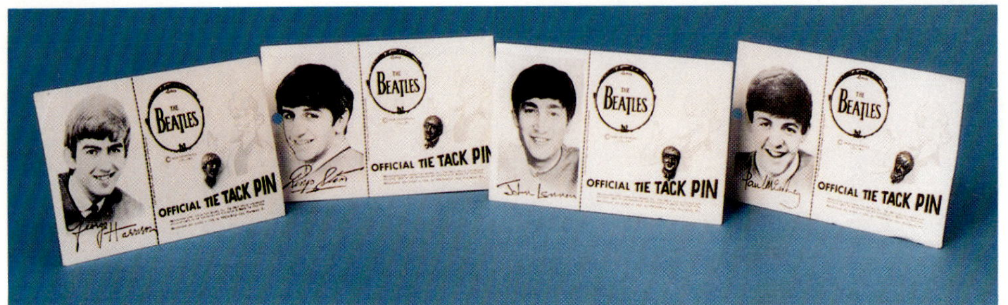

Plate 315. *Beatles Tie Tac Pins*. Good, $80.00; Excellent/Mint, $95.00.

Plate 316. *Beatles Celebrity Novelty Bracelet*. Good, $200.00; Excellent/Mint, $215.00. *Beatles Photo Necklace*. Good, $170.00; Excellent/Mint, $180.00.

Plate 317. *Beatles Tie Tac Pin Group with Guitar*. Good, $110.00; Excellent/Mint, $115.00.

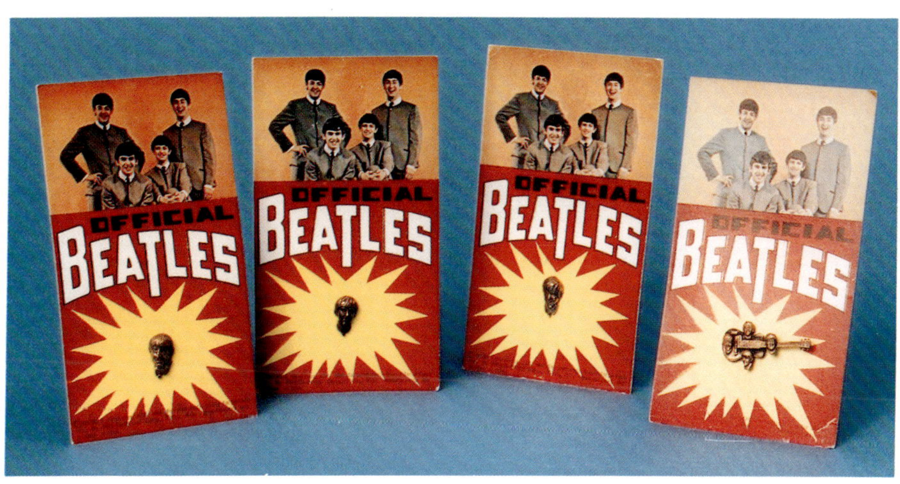

Plate 318. *Beatles Tie Tacs on Colored Cards*. Good, $90.00; Excellent/Mint, $100.00.

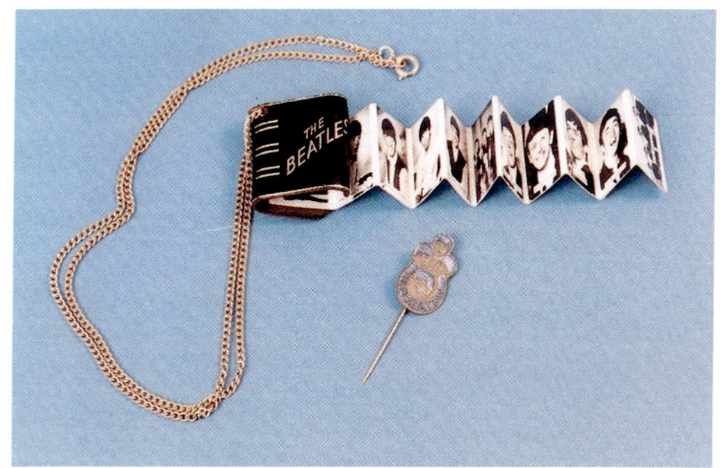

Plate 319. *Photo Necklace*. Good, $80.00; Excellent/Mint, $85.00. *Stick Pin*. Good, $45.00; Excellent/Mint, $50.00.

Plate 320. *Aluminum Key Chain*. Good, $60.00; Excellent/Mint, $65.00. *Flasher Bracelet*. Good, $60.00; Excellent/Mint, $65.00.

Plate 321. *Flasher Rings*. Good, $10.00; Excellent/Mint, $15.00.

Plate 322. *Flasher Rings Display Card*. Good, $700.00; Excellent/Mint, $750.00.

Plate 323. *Beatles Tie Tacs* were made by Press-Initial Corporation. Good, $85.00; Excellent/Mint, $95.00.

Plate 324. *Beatle Tac*. Good, $70.00; Excellent/Mint, $75.00.

Plate 325. *Assorted Beatle Jewelry*. Good, $30.00; Excellent/Mint, $40.00.

Plate 326. *Beatle Pin*. Good, $130.00; Excellent/Mint, $135.00.

Plate 327. *Beatle Bracelet*. Good, $125.00; Excellent/Mint, $135.00. *Record Necklace*. Good, $85.00; Excellent/Mint, $95.00. *Belt Buckle*. Good, $175.00; Excellent/Mint, $200.00. *Photo Key Chain*. Good, $70.00; Excellent/Mint, $80.00.

Plate 328. *Beatle Bracelet* produced by Randall. Good, $225.00; Excellent/Mint, $250.00.

Plate 329. *Beatle Pin*. Good, $110.00; Excellent/Mint, $115.00. *Photo Pin*. Good, $110.00; Excellent/Mint, $115.00. *Necklace*. Good, $70.00; Excellent/Mint, $75.00. *"B" Pin*. Good, $150.00; Excellent/Mint, $160.00. *Four Headed Necklace*. Good, $50.00; Excellent/Mint, $55.00. *Beatle Locket*. Good, $70.00; Excellent/Mint, $75.00. *Beatle Bracelet*. Good, $160.00; Excellent/Mint, $165.00.

Plate 330. *Bracelet*. Good, $110.00; Excellent/Mint, $115.00. *Pin*. Good, $125.00; Excellent/Mint, $130.00. *Beatle Locket*. Good, $80.00; Excellent/Mint, $90.00. *Beatle Pin with Guitar and Drum*. Good, $160.00; Excellent/Mint, $175.00. *Large Beatle Necklace*. Good, $200.00; Excellent/Mint, $210.00.

Plate 331. *Beatle Seltaeb Ceramic Bracelet*. Good, $180.00; Excellent/Mint, $190.00. *Beatle Seltaeb Ceramic Necklace*. Good, $180.00; Excellent/Mint, $190.00.

Plate 332. *Randall Necklace*. Good, $200.00; Excellent/Mint, $225.00. *Randall Necklace*. Good, $170.00; Excellent/Mint, $180.00. *Randall Bracelet*. Good, $170.00; Excellent/Mint, $180.00.

Plate 333. *Beatles Jewelry Brooches.* Good, $70.00; Excellent/Mint, $75.00.

Plate 334. *Beatles Jewelry Brooches.* Good, $70.00; Excellent/Mint, $75.00.

Plate 335. *Beatles Record Necklace.* Good, $125.00; Excellent/Mint, $135.00.

Plate 336. *Beatles Invicta Plastic Guitar Brooches on Large Card.* Good, $125.00; Excellent/Mint, $130.00.

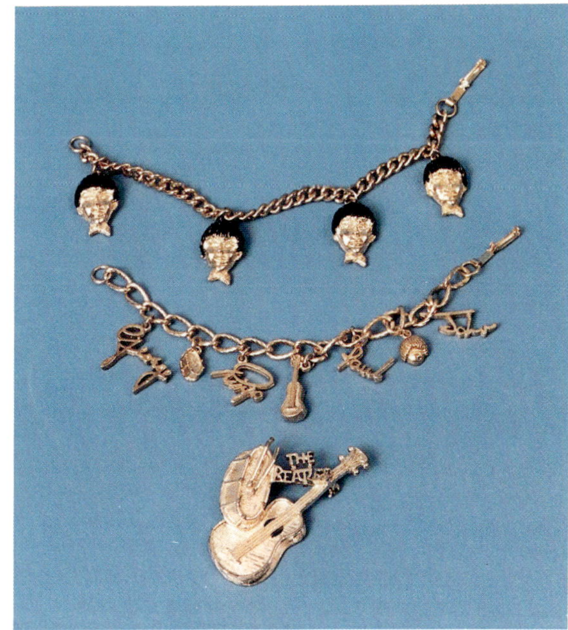

Plate 337. *Bracelet.* Good, $70.00; Excellent/Mint, $80.00. *Charm Bracelet.* Good, $130.00; Excellent/Mint, $135.00. *Drum and Guitar Pin.* Good, $140.00; Excellent/Mint, $150.00.

Plate 338. *Beatle Brooch.* Good, $115.00; Excellent/Mint, $120.00; *Beatle Brooch on Card.* Good, $200.00; Excellent/Mint, $220.00.

Plate 339. *Beatle Bracelet.* Good, $90.00; Excellent/Mint, $110.00. *Beatle Necklace.* Good, $90.00; Excellent/Mint, $110.00.

CHAPTER THREE
Yellow Submarine

In 1968, the Beatles completed their animated feature "Yellow Submarine." This gave them another marketing licensing bonanza. A whole new array of merchandise was produced to immortalize the movie. Cartoon characters like the Blue Meanie and Jeremy the Boob were utilized to produce different and new items.

The Yellow Submarine memorabilia is coveted today because of its vibrant colors and exciting images.

Metal Yellow Submarine Lunch Box.

Plate 340. *Alarm Clock* was produced by Sheffield Watch Company. It is very hard to find in working order. Good, $900.00; Excellent/Mint, $1,000.00.

Plate 341. *Banks* were made by Pride Creations. They are marked with a sticker on the bottom of each figure. They are about 8" tall. Good, $1,700.00; Excellent/Mint, $1,900.00.

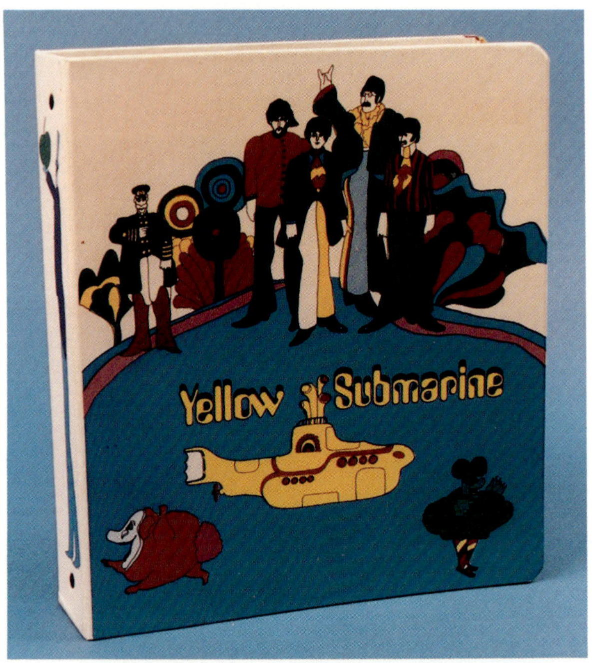

Plate 342. *Binder* was made by Vernon Royal. This was the only style binder created. Good, $200.00; Excellent/Mint, $225.00.

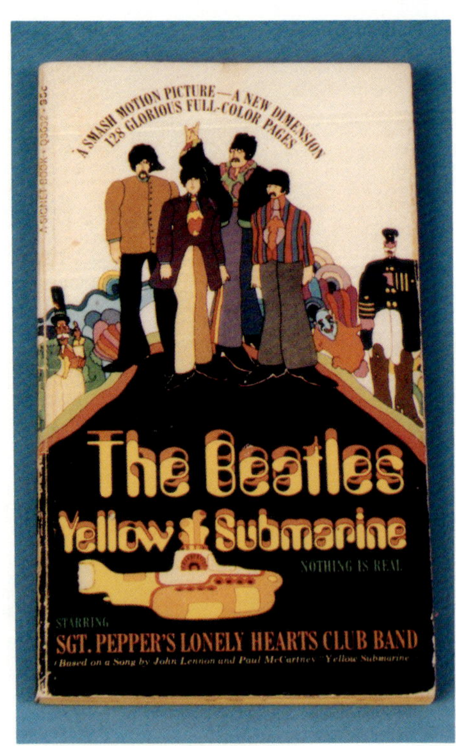

Plate 343. *Book* was published by Signet and is a paperback book. Good, $5.00; Excellent/Mint, $10.00.

Plate 344. *Book Markers* were made of the various yellow submarine characters. Good, $10.00; Excellent/Mint, $12.00.

Plate 345. *Bulletin Boards* were made by Unicorn Creations. The Head Meanie is shown here in its original packaging. Good, $125.00; Excellent/Mint, $140.00.

Plate 347. *Bulletin Board* (Snapping Turk). Good, $125.00; Excellent/Mint, $140.00.

Plate 346. *Bulletin Board* (Stamp Out Fun). Good, $125.00; Excellent/Mint, $140.00.

Plate 348. *Bulletin Board* which is the hardest to find is pictured here showing all the Beatles. Good, $175.00; Excellent/Mint, $200.00.

Plate 349. *Buttons*. Good, $8.00; Excellent/Mint, $10.00.

Plate 350. *Buttons* made with Yellow Sub sayings. Good, $10.00; Excellent/Mint, $12.00.

Plate 351. *Calendar* was produced by Golden Press. It is spiral bound. Each month displays a different movie scene. Good, $125.00; Excellent/Mint, $150.00.

Plate 352. *Candle* is encased in a glass cylinder. This item is one of the rarest Yellow Submarine items. Good, $600.00; Excellent/Mint, $625.00.

Plate 353. *Cereal Boxes* graphics were on the back of Wheat and Rice Honeys and were used to advertise rub-ons. Good, $1,200.00; Excellent/Mint, $1,400.00.

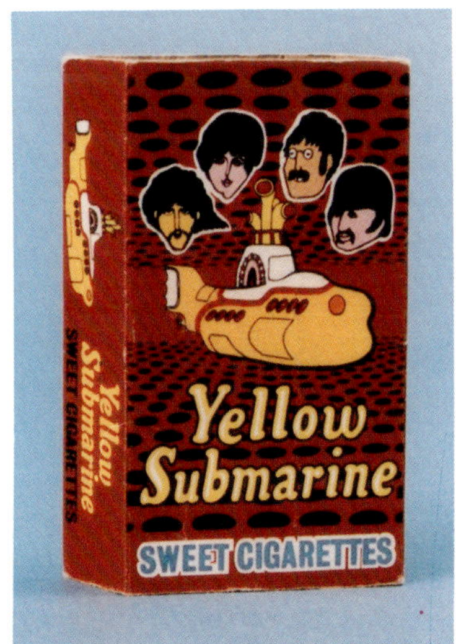

Plate 354. *Cigarettes* were made by Primrose Confectionary. The box contained 10 candy cigarettes. Good, $130.00; Excellent/Mint, $140.00.

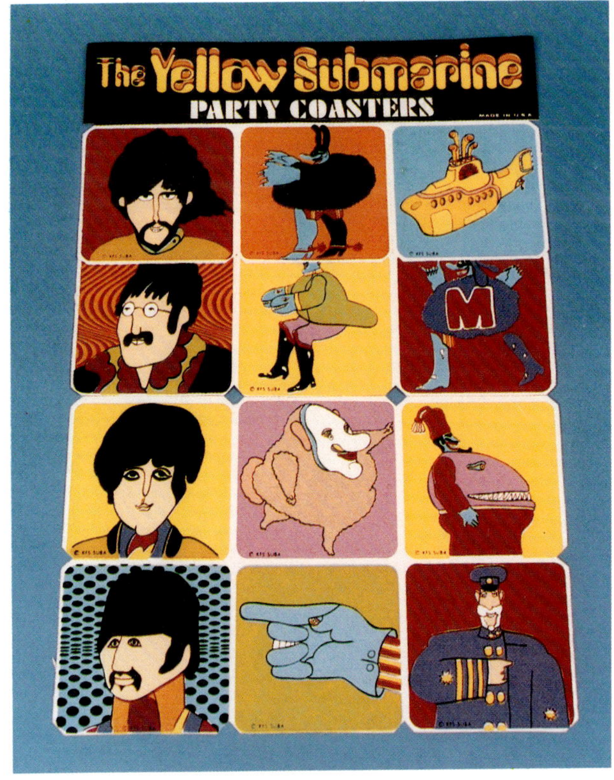

Plate 355. *Coasters* were made by K. Cennar and were manufactured in twelve different coasters. Good, $100.00; Excellent/Mint, $115.00.

Plate 356. *Dimensionals* were made by Craft Master Paper. When constructed, it makes a colorful wall hanging. Good, $300.00; Excellent/Mint, $325.00.

Plate 357. *Greeting Cards* came in a variety of boxes. Good, $130.00; Excellent/Mint, $140.00.

Plate 358. *Greeting Cards* were made by Sunshine Card Company. Good, $130.00; Excellent/Mint, $140.00.

Plate 359. *Greeting Cards* displayed scenes from the Yellow Submarine movie. Good, $130.00; Excellent/Mint, $140.00.

Plate 360. *Halloween Costume* was made by Collegeville Costumes. The Blue Meanie was the only character costume produced. Good, $400.00; Excellent/Mint, $425.00.

Plate 361. *Hanger* (Paul) was made by Henderson-Haggard, Inc. The hanger is 16" tall. Good, $100.00; Excellent/Mint, $120.00.

Plate 362. *Hanger* (John). Good, $100.00; Excellent/Mint, $120.00.

Plate 363. *Hanger* (George). Good, $100.00; Excellent/Mint, $120.00.

Plate 364. *Hanger* (Ringo) has the image on both sides. Good, $100.00; Excellent/Mint, $120.00.

Plate 365. *Keychains* were made by Pride Creations. Good, $8.00; Excellent/Mint, $10.00.

Plate 366. *Keychains* were made by Pride Creations. Good, $20.00; Excellent/Mint, $25.00.

Plate 367. *Lobby Cards* were used with the release of Yellow Submarine. These are the rarer British versions. Good, $500.00; Excellent/Mint, $525.00.

Plate 368. *Lobby Cards* are marked King Features – Subafilms, Ltd. Good, $500.00; Excellent/Mint, $525.00.

Plate 369. *Lunchbox* was made by King Seeley. The thermos pictured accompanied the lunch box. Good, $300.00; Excellent/Mint, $375.00.

Plate 370. *Mobile* was made by Sunshine Art Studios. When assembled, figures are connected by a black string. Good, $220.00; Excellent/Mint, $230.00.

Plate 371. *Model* was made by Model Products Corporation. It came with plastic Beatles. Good, $260.00; Excellent/Mint, $275.00.

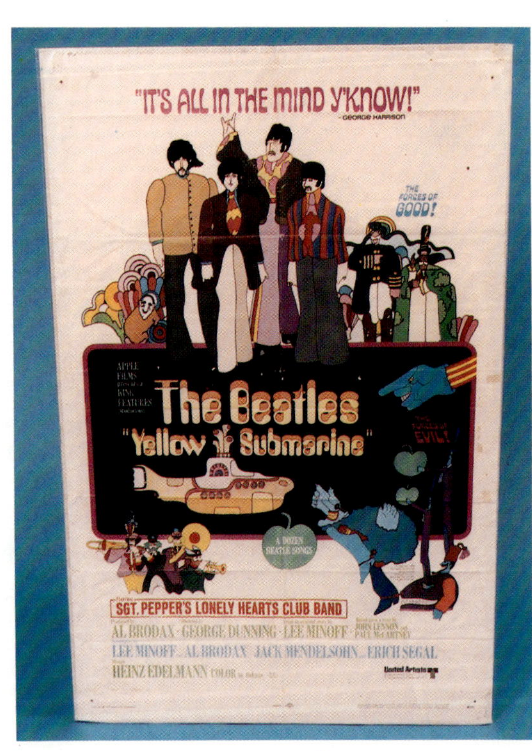

Plate 372. *Movie Poster* is the one sheet used in theater's lobby. Good, $240.00; Excellent/Mint, $260.00.

Plate 373. *Notebooks* were made by Vernon Royal and show the two spiral bound sizes produced. Good, $130.00; Excellent/Mint, $150.00.

Plate 374. *Pencil Holder* is one of the harder to find Yellow Sub items. Good, $400.00; Excellent/Mint, $425.00.

Plate 375. *Photo Album* is the smaller version that could hold 12 photos and came with a small plastic case. Good, $325.00; Excellent/Mint, $350.00.

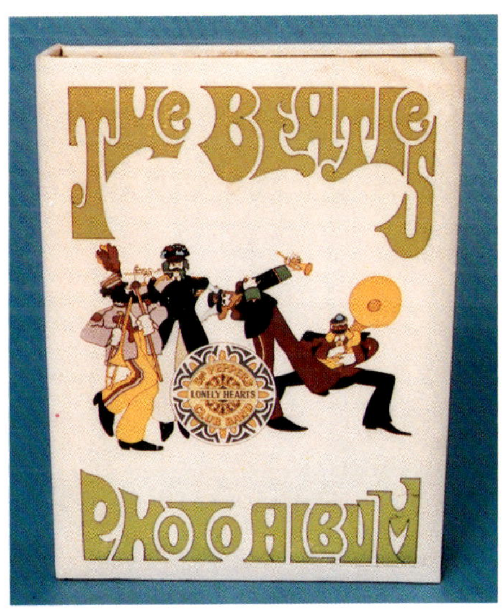

Plate 376. *Photo Album* is the larger size. Good, $400.00; Excellent/Mint, $425.00.

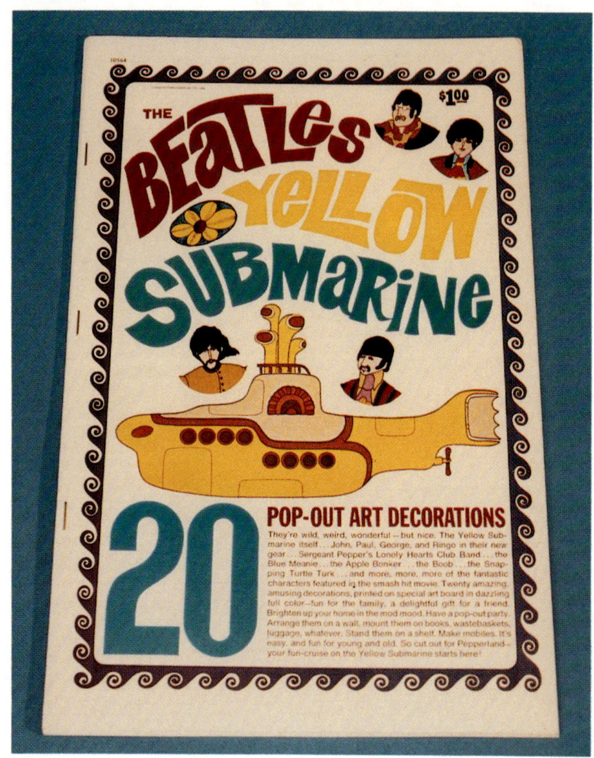

Plate 377. *Pop-outs* are art decorations. Good, $30.00; Excellent/Mint, $35.00.

Plate 378. *Put-Ons* were made by Craft Master. There were 60 stickers that attached to the poster included. Good, $200.00; Excellent/Mint, $225.00.

Plate 379. *Postcards*. Good, $60.00. Excellent/Mint, $65.00.

Plate 380. *Puzzle* (In the Yellow Sub) has 650 pieces and measures 19" x 19". Good, $125.00; Excellent/Mint, $150.00.

Plate 381. *Puzzle* (Sgt. Pepper Band) has 160 pieces and was made by Jaymar. Good, $100.00; Excellent/Mint, $125.00.

Plate 382. *Puzzle* (Sea of Monsters) has over 650 pieces and is 19" x 19". Good, $125.00; Excellent/Mint, $150.00.

Plate 383. *Puzzle* (Sgt. Pepper Band) has over 650 pieces and is 19" x 19". Good, $125.00; Excellent/Mint, $150.00.

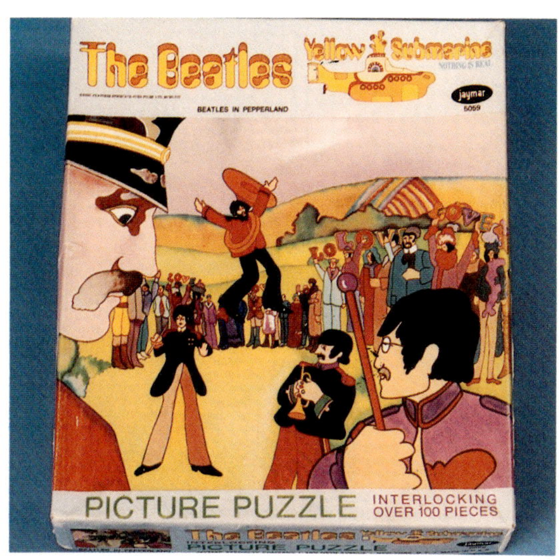

Plate 384. *Puzzle* (Beatles in Pepperland). Good, $100.00; Excellent/Mint, $125.00.

Plate 385. *Puzzle* (Sea of Monsters) has over 100 interlocking pieces. Good, $100.00; Excellent/Mint, $125.00.

Plate 386. *Puzzle* (Meanies Invade Pepperland). Good, $125.00; Excellent/Mint, $150.00.

Plate 387. *Puzzle* (Blue Meanies Attack). Good, $125.00; Excellent/Mint, $150.00.

Plate 388. *Puzzle* (Beatles in Pepperland) is an example of the Bantam Pocket Puzzle. Good, $115.00; Excellent/Mint, $125.00.

Plate 389. *Rub-ons* were distributed in cereal boxes. There were eight different sheets; all with various character combinations. Good, $15.00; Excellent/Mint, $20.00 each.

Plate 390. *Stationery* was manufactured by Unicorn Creations. Good, $135.00. Excellent/Mint, $150.00.

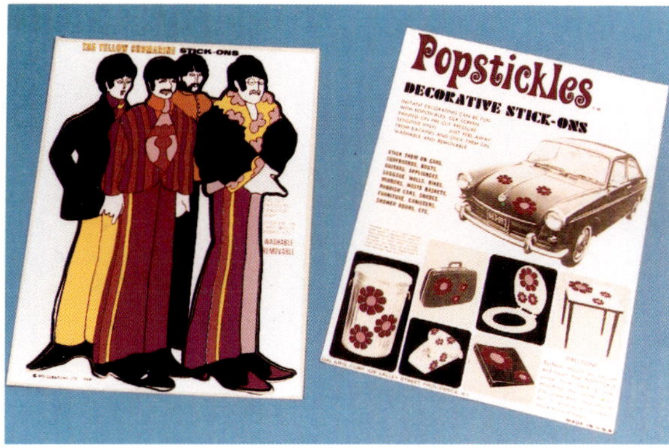

Plate 391. *Stick-ons* were made by Dal Manufacturing Corporation and came with instruction sheet suggesting good places to stick them. Good, $75.00; Excellent/Mint, $80.00.

Plate 392. *Stick-ons*. Good, $75.00; Excellent/Mint, $80.00.

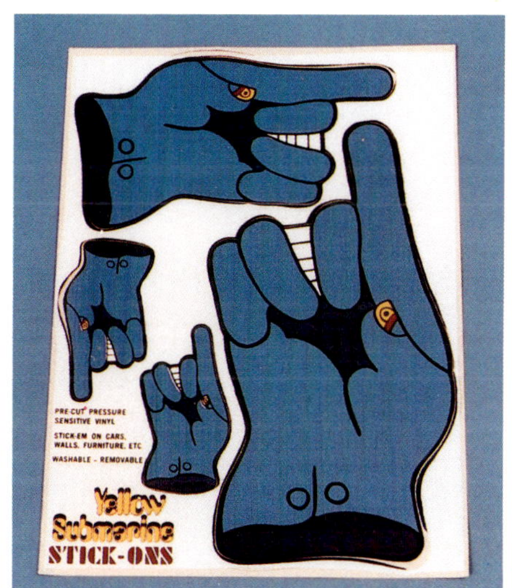

Plate 393. *Stick-ons*. Good, $75.00; Excellent/Mint, $80.00.

Plate 394. *Switch Plate Covers* were made by Dal Manufacturing Corporation. They are heavy cardboard. Good, $70.00; Excellent/Mint, $75.00 each.

Plate 395. *Submarine* was made by Corgi. It is made of metal and measures 5¼" long. Good, $400.00; Excellent/Mint, $425.00.

Plate 396. *Tie Tac Pin* was licensed by King Feature Syndicate. Good, $70.00; Excellent/Mint, $80.00.

Plate 397. *Wall Plaque* (Paul) is made of cardboard and is used to hang on the wall. Good, $125.00; Excellent/Mint, $150.00.

Plate 398. *Wall Plaque* (George). Good, $125.00; Excellent/Mint, $150.00.

Plate 399. *Wall Plaque* (John). Good, $125.00; Excellent/Mint, $150.00.

Plate 400. *Wall Plaque* (Ringo). Good, $125.00; Excellent/Mint, $150.00.

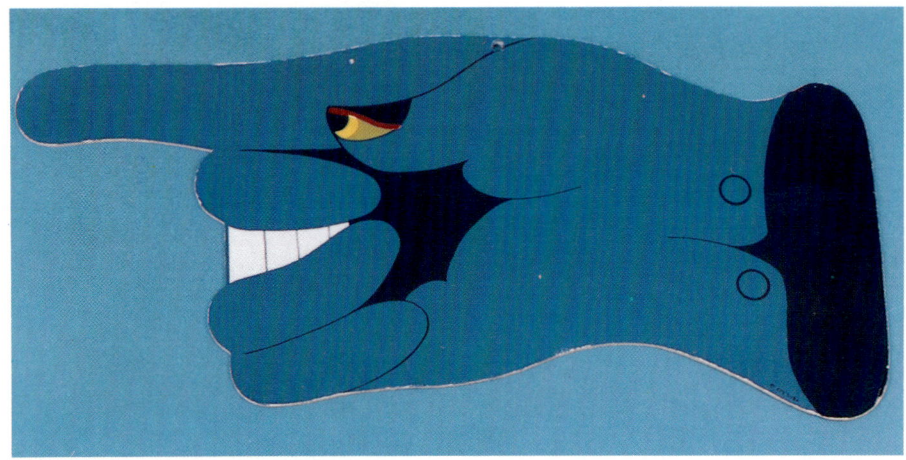

Plate 401. *Wall Plaque* (Glove). Good, $125.00; Excellent/Mint, $150.00.

Plate 402. *Water Color Set* was made by Craft Master. Good, $135.00; Excellent/Mint, $145.00.

Plate 403. *Water Color Set* came with six 8 x 10 pictures. Good, $145.00; Excellent/Mint, $155.00.

Yellow Submarine Celluloids

The collecting of celluloids from the movie *Yellow Submarine* is fast becoming one of the most popular areas of Beatles memorabilia. The prices of the cels are increasing at a rapid rate. In the field of Disneyana, cels have always brought the highest prices at auctions.

A cel is a painting on celluloid by studio artists of an animated character or object. It is based on the artist's original pencil drawing. Cels in many cases are shown with backgrounds which were photographed during the productions of the final released versions of a film.

The only original celluloids from the Beatles era are from the only animation feature — the *Yellow Submarine*. Cels featuring one or more Beatles command much higher prices. A cel showing the yellow submarine is the rarest and most difficult to find.

Plate 404. *Dancing Man*. Good, $350.00; Excellent/Mint, $400.00.

Plate 405. *Ringo with Doors*. Good, $1,200.00; Excellent/Mint, $1,500.00.

Plate 406. *Flying Paul.* Good, $850.00; Excellent/Mint, $900.00.

Plate 407. *Ringo and Paul and Stone People*. Good, $850.00; Excellent/Mint, $950.00.

Plate 409. *Meanie with Apple and Max*. Good, $600.00; Excellent/Mint, $625.00.

Plate 408. *Captain Old Fred*. Good, $400.00; Excellent/Mint, $450.00.

Plate 410. *Paul with Apples*. Good, $800.00; Excellent/Mint, $850.00.

Plate 411. *Policeman*. Good, $400.00; Excellent/Mint, $425.00.

Plate 412. *Jeremy the Boob*. Good, $350.00; Excellent/Mint, $375.00.

Plate 413. *Jeremy with Plane Propeller*. Good, $275.00; Excellent/Mint, $300.00.

Plate 414. *Max*. Good, $600.00; Excellent/Mint, $625.00.

Plate 415. *Max*. Good, $1,100.00; Excellent/Mint, $1,200.00.

Plate 416. *Max*. Good, $700.00; Excellent/Mint, $725.00.

Plate 417. *Ringo with Rainbow*. Good, $1,250.00; Excellent/Mint, $1,350.00.

Plate 418. *Ringo with Original Background*. Good, $2,500.00; Excellent/Mint, $2,800.00.

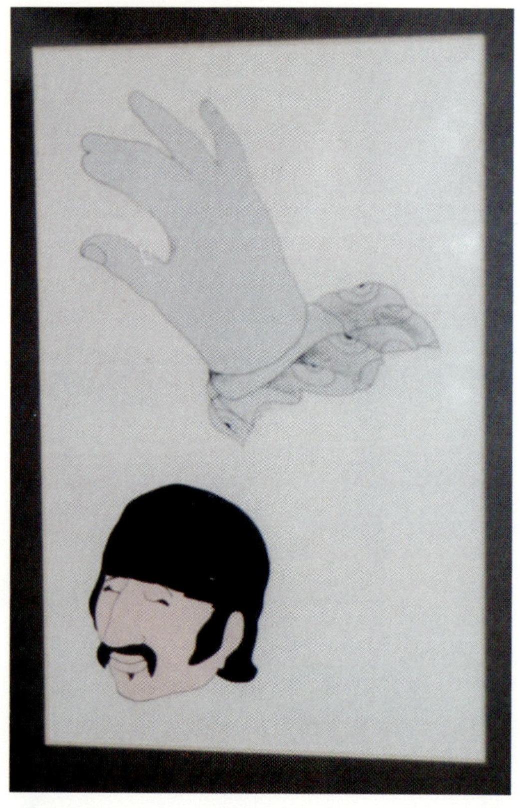

Plate 419. *Ringo with Hand*. Good, $1,000.00; Excellent/Mint, $1,150.00.

Plate 420. *John with Policeman*. Good, $1,100.00; Excellent/Mint, $1,200.00.

CHAPTER FOUR
Apple Studio

Promotional items produced by Apple Studios are very collectible. Many were produced in limited numbers and some were given as gifts making them exceedingly rare.

Most Apple items were used as promotional pieces and were not designed for retail sale. An Apple memento value is based more along the pricing of a personal Beatle piece.

Plate 421. *Brass Apple* was given out at the opening of Apple Studios. It is believed that there were one hundred of these produced. Good. $2,000.00; Excellent/Mint, $2,200.00.

Plate 422. *Cube* was sent by Apple Records as part of a fan club promotion. Good, $40.00; Excellent/Mint, $45.00.

Plate 423. *Merry Christmas Apple* is made of foam rubber and was given out as a Christmas gift by the studio. Good, $1,800.00; Excellent/Mint, $2,000.00.

Plate 425. *Stickers* used by Apple with theme "Stick a garden on something you love." Good, $70.00; Excellent/Mint, $75.00.

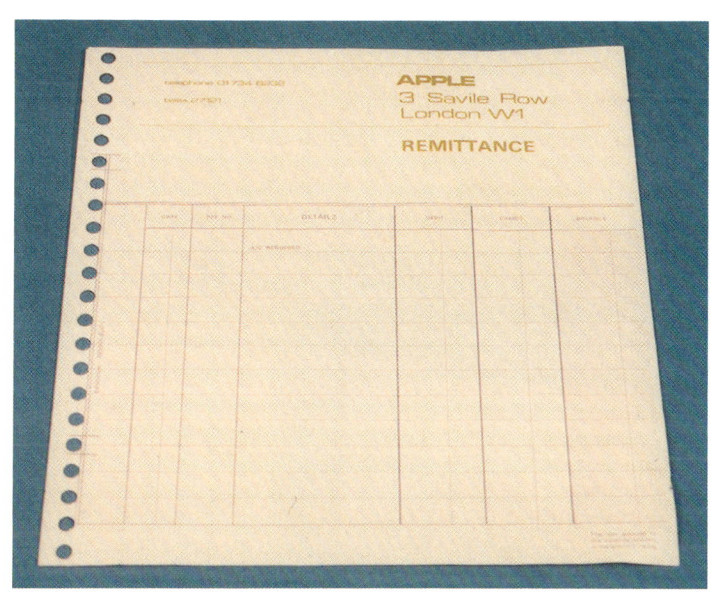

APPLE
3 Savile Row
London W1

REMITTANCE

DETAILS

Plate 424. *Remittance* is an actual form used by Apple Studio to record their artists' expenses. Good, $60.00; Excellent/Mint, $65.00.

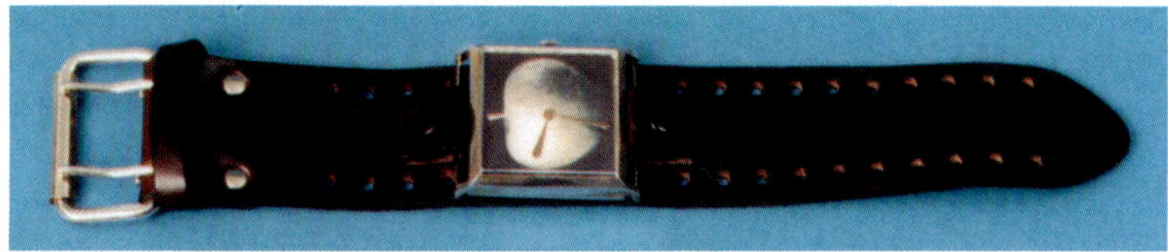

Plate 426. *Watch* has green apple logo on the face and has a black leather band. Good, $1,000.00; Excellent/Mint, $1,100.00.

CHAPTER FIVE
One of a Kind Items

This chapter deals with items that are considered one-of-a-kind. There are collectors who want only items owned and used by the Beatles. These include automobiles, musical instruments, and clothing. Another field is Beatle autographs, and prices vary greatly on the particular item or piece of paper the autographs were written on.

Gold records given to the Beatles, or one of their organizations or record companies, are also an area that collectors utilize. Beware of forgeries and reproductions. Make sure you receive documentation that your item is genuine.

Plate 427. *Beatles Autographs* and Gerry and the Pacemakers autographs. Good, $1,700.00; Excellent/Mint, $1,800.00.

Photo 428. *Yellow Submarine Gold Record* presented to John Lennon. This is exceedingly rare because it was presented to an actual Beatle. Note the white mat which is indicative of its value. Good, $13,000.00; Excellent/Mint, $15,000.00.

Plate 429. *Plastic Ono Band Gold Record* is not as rare because it came after the Beatles broke up. Good, $2,500.00; Excellent/Mint, $4,000.00.

Plate 430. *John Lennon Suit*. Good, $10,000.00; Excellent/Mint, $11,000.00.

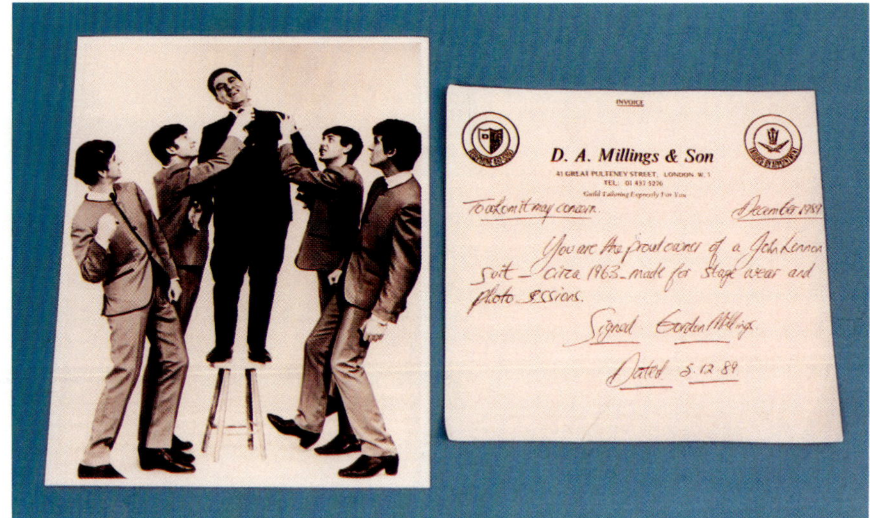

INVOICE

D. A. Millings & Son

41 GREAT PULTENEY STREET, LONDON W.1

TEL: 01 437 5276

Guild Tailoring Expressly For You

To whom it may concern. December 1989

You are the proud owner of a John Lennon suit – circa 1963 – made for stage wear and photo sessions.

Signed Gordon Millings

Dated 5.12.89

Plate 431. *Letter of Authenticity* from D.A. Millings and Son, the original tailor.

Collector Resources

The field of Beatle collectors is growing and the intensity of these Beatles enthusiasts is overwhelming. Many publications and auction catalogs are available for those wishing to acquire Beatles memorabilia through the mail. The following are publications that contain valuable information on a variety of Beatle topics.

Mark Lapidos Productions
P.O. Box 436
Westwood, NJ 07675-0436

GOOD DAY SUNSHINE
397 Edgewood Ave.
New Haven, CT 06511

Beatles Unlimited Magazine
P.O. Box 602 — 3430AP Nievwegern
The Netherlands

The following are reputable phone bid auction houses that deal in Beatles:

BOJO
P.O. Box 1203
Cranberry Turnpike, PA 16033-2203

Steve Witt
17233 East 41st Street
Independence, MO 64055

New England Auction Gallery
P.O. Box 2273
W. Peabody, MA 01960-7273

Hake's Americana Collectibles
P.O. Box 1444
York, PA 17405

Author Profiles

Michael Stern

Barbara Crawford

Hollis Lamon

Michael Stern is author of three price guides on Disney toys, *Stern's Guide to Disney Collectibles, First and Second Series,* and the *Collector's Encyclopedia of Disneyana.* He is a financial advisor with Lamon & Stern and runs a stock hedge funds called Zenith. Michael resides in Atlanta, Georgia, with his wife Merrill and twin daughters, Jenny and Lisa. If you have Beatle items to sell or trade, contact him at: 1950 North Park Place, Suite 100, Atlanta, GA 30339.

Barbara Crawford did all the excellent photography in the book. She is also the proud owner of all the items pictured in this book. Barbara lives in Atlanta, Georgia, with her four dogs and four cats. Barbara has always been an avid Beatle fan. She has almost every piece of recorded music that they have done.

Hollis Lamon is a partner with Michael Stern in Lamon & Stern. He is a financial advisor. He is also one of the leading collectors of Yoda Memorabilia in the country. Hollis lives in Atlanta with his wife, Jane, and his two sons, Hunter and Austin.

The authors wish to thank Collector Books for making a dream become a reality. We are already working on Volume Two and desire to purchase any items not found in this volume. Please call or write:

Michael Stern
1950 North Park Place, Suite 100
Atlanta, GA 30339
404/951-8411

Books on Antiques and Collectibles

This is only a partial listing of the books on antiques that are available from Collector Books. All books are well illustrated and contain current values. Most of the following books are available from your local book seller or antique dealer, or from your public library. If you are unable to locate certain titles in your area you may order by mail from COLLECTOR BOOKS, P.O. Box 3009, Paducah, KY 42002-3009. Customers with Visa or MasterCard may phone in orders from 8:00-4:00 CST, M-F – Toll Free 1-800-626-5420. Add $2.00 for postage for the first book ordered and $.30 for each additional book. Include item number, title and price when ordering. Allow 14 to 21 days for delivery.

BOOKS ON GLASS AND POTTERY

1810 American Art Glass, Shuman $29.95
2016 Bedroom & Bathroom Glassware of the Depression Years $19.95
1312 Blue & White Stoneware, McNerney $9.95
1959 Blue Willow, 2nd Ed., Gaston $14.95
3719 Coll. Glassware from the 40's, 50's, 60's, 2nd Ed., Florence $19.95
3311 Collecting Yellow Ware - Id. & Value Gd., McAllister $16.95
2352 Collector's Ency. of Akro Agate Glassware, Florence $14.95
1373 Collector's Ency. of American Dinnerware, Cunningham $24.95
2272 Collector's Ency. of California Pottery, Chipman $24.95
3312 Collector's Ency. of Children's Dishes, Whitmyer $19.95
2133 Collector's Ency. of Cookie Jars, Roerig $24.95
3724 Collector's Ency. of Depression Glass, 11th Ed., Florence $19.95
2209 Collector's Ency. of Fiesta, 7th Ed., Huxford $19.95
1439 Collector's Ency. of Flow Blue China, Gaston $19.95
1915 Collector's Ency. of Hall China, 2nd Ed., Whitmyer $19.95
2334 Collector's Ency. of Majolica Pottery, Katz-Marks $19.95
1358 Collector's Ency. of McCoy Pottery, Huxford $19.95
3313 Collector's Ency. of Niloak, Gifford $19.95
3433 Collector's Guide To Harker Pottery - U.S.A., Colbert $17.95
1039 Collector's Ency. of Nippon Porcelain I, Van Patten $19.95
2089 Collector's Ency. of Nippon Porcelain II, Van Patten $24.95
1665 Collector's Ency. of Nippon Porcelain III, Van Patten $24.95
1447 Collector's Ency. of Noritake, 1st Series, Van Patten $19.95
1034 Collector's Ency. of Roseville Pottery, Huxford $19.95
1035 Collector's Ency. of Roseville Pottery, 2nd Ed., Huxford $19.95
3314 Collector's Ency. of Van Briggle Art Pottery, Sasicki $24.95
2339 Collector's Guide to Shawnee Pottery, Vanderbilt $19.95
1425 Cookie Jars, Westfall $9.95
3440 Cookie Jars, Book II, Westfall $19.95
2275 Czechoslovakian Glass & Collectibles, Barta $16.95
3315 Elegant Glassware of the Depression Era, 5th Ed., Florence $19.95
3318 Glass Animals of the Depression Era, Garmon & Spencer $19.95
2024 Kitchen Glassware of the Depression Years, 4th Ed., Florence $19.95
3322 Pocket Guide to Depression Glass, 8th Ed., Florence $9.95
1670 Red Wing Collectibles, DePasquale $9.95
1440 Red Wing Stoneware, DePasquale $9.95
1958 So. Potteries Blue Ridge Dinnerware, 3rd Ed., Newbound $14.95
3739 Standard Carnival Glass, 4th Ed., Edwards $24.95
1848 Very Rare Glassware of the Depression Years, Florence $24.95
2140 Very Rare Glassware of the Depression Years, Second Series $24.95
3326 Very Rare Glassware of the Depression Era, Third Series $24.95
3327 Watt Pottery - Identification & Value Guide, Morris $19.95
2224 World of Salt Shakers, 2nd Ed., Lechner $24.95

BOOKS ON DOLLS & TOYS

2079 Barbie Fashion, Vol. 1, 1959-1967, Eames $24.95
3310 Black Dolls - 1820-1991 - Id. & Value Guide, Perkins $17.95
1514 Character Toys & Collectibles 1st Series, Longest $19.95
1750 Character Toys & Collectibles, 2nd Series, Longest $19.95
1529 Collector's Ency. of Barbie Dolls, DeWein $19.95
2338 Collector's Ency. of Disneyana, Longest & Stern $24.95
3441 Madame Alexander Price Guide #18, Smith $9.95
1540 Modern Toys, 1930-1980, Baker $19.95
3442 Patricia Smith's Doll Values Antique to Modern, 9th ed $12.95
1886 Stern's Guide to Disney $14.95
2139 Stern's Guide to Disney, 2nd Series $14.95
1513 Teddy Bears & Steiff Animals, Mandel $9.95
1817 Teddy Bears & Steiff Animals, 2nd, Mandel $19.95
2084 Teddy Bears, Annalees & Steiff Animals, 3rd, Mandel $19.95
2028 Toys, Antique & Collectible, Longest $14.95
1808 Wonder of Barbie, Manos $9.95
1430 World of Barbie Dolls, Manos $9.95

OTHER COLLECTIBLES

1457 American Oak Furniture, McNerney $9.95
2269 Antique Brass & Copper, Gaston $16.95
2333 Antique & Collectible Marbles, 3rd Ed., Grist, ... $9.95
1712 Antique & Collectible Thimbles, Mathis $19.95
1748 Antique Purses, Holiner $19.95
1868 Antique Tools, Our American Heritage, McNerney $9.95
1426 Arrowheads & Projectile Points, Hothem $7.95
1278 Art Nouveau & Art Deco Jewelry, Baker $9.95
1714 Black Collectibles, Gibbs $19.95
1128 Bottle Pricing Guide, 3rd Ed., Cleveland $7.95
1752 Christmas Ornaments, Johnston $19.95
2132 Collector's Ency. of American Furniture, Vol. I, Swedberg $24.95
2271 Collector's Ency. of American Furniture, Vol. II, Swedberg $24.95
2018 Collector's Ency. of Graniteware, Greguire $24.95
3430 Coll. Ency. of Granite Ware, Book II, Greguire $24.95
2083 Collector's Ency. of Russel Wright Designs, Kerr $19.95
2337 Collector's Guide to Decoys, Book II, Huxford $16.95
2340 Collector's Guide to Easter Collectibles, Burnett $16.95
1441 Collector's Guide to Post Cards, Wood $9.95
2276 Decoys, Kangas $24.95
1629 Doorstops, Id. & Values, Bertoia $9.95
1716 Fifty Years of Fashion Jewelry, Baker $19.95
3316 Flea Market Trader, 8th Ed., Huxford $9.95
3317 Florence's Standard Baseball Card Price Gd., 5th Ed. $9.95
1755 Furniture of the Depression Era, Swedberg $19.95
3436 Grist's Big Book of Marbles, Everett Grist $19.95
2278 Grist's Machine Made & Contemporary Marbles $9.95
1424 Hatpins & Hatpin Holders, Baker $9.95
3319 Huxford's Collectible Advertising - Id. & Value Gd. $17.95
3439 Huxford's Old Book Value Guide, 5th Ed. $19.95
1181 100 Years of Collectible Jewelry, Baker $9.95
2023 Keen Kutter Collectibles, 2nd Ed., Heuring $14.95
2216 Kitchen Antiques - 1790–1940, McNerney $14.95
3320 Modern Guns - Id. & Val. Gd., 9th Ed., Quertermous $12.95
1965 Pine Furniture, Our Am. Heritage, McNerney $14.95
3321 Ornamental & Figural Nutcrackers, Rittenhouse $16.95
2026 Railroad Collectibles, 4th Ed., Baker $14.95
1632 Salt & Pepper Shakers, Guarnaccia $9.95
1888 Salt & Pepper Shakers II, Guarnaccia $14.95
2220 Salt & Pepper Shakers III, Guarnaccia $14.95
3443 Salt & Pepper Shakers IV, Guarnaccia $18.95
3737 Schroeder's Antiques Price Guide, 12th Ed. $12.95
2096 Silverplated Flatware, 4th Ed., Hagan $14.95
3325 Standard Knife Collector's Guide, Stewart $12.95
2348 20th Century Fashionable Plastic Jewelry, Baker $19.95
3444 Wanted To Buy, 4th Ed. $9.95

Schr... ...es

...ues *Price Guide* ...usehold name in ...ctibles field. Our ... year-round with ...utors to bring you ...ok on antiques &

...000 items identi- ...*er's* is a must for ... alike. If it merits ... collector, you'll ... Each subject is ...ries and back- ... addition, hun- ...photos are used ... not only the rare and unusual, but the everyday "fun-type" collectibles as well -- not postage stamp pictures, but large close-up shots that show important details clearly.

Our editors compile a new book each year. Never do we merely change prices. Accuracy is our primary aim. Prices are gathered over the entire year previous to publication, from ads and personal contacts. Then each category is thoroughly checked to spot inconsistencies, listings that may not be entirely reflective of actual market dealings, and lines too vague to be of merit. Only the best of the lot remains for publication. You'll find *Schroeder's Antiques Price Guide* the one to buy for factual information and quality.

No dealer, collector or investor can afford not to own this book. It is available from your favorite bookseller or antiques dealer at the low price of $12.95. If you are unable to find this price guide in your area, it's available from Collector Books, P.O. Box 3009, Paducah, KY 42002-3009 at $12.95 plus $2.00 for postage and handling.

8½ x 11", 608 Pages **$12.95**

COLLECTOR BOOKS

A Division of Schroeder Publishing Co., Inc.